Spirit
Dance

Spirit Dance

Discovering the Power of God's Grace

Margaret Westphal

MWIM Productions
Tulsa, OK

To my father
James Howard Cross
who went to be with the Lord October 12, 2002
and
my father-in-law
Cloyd Robert Westphal
who went to be with the Lord May 21, 2002

They both went to heaven during the time of the final editing of this book.
How we love and miss them.
I dedicate this book to them and to all the precious people who are my family

The family I was born into

The family I married into

The family that the Lord gave to me: my husband Russell
Our daughter Rachael
Our son Chad
Our daughter-in-law Amy
Our daughter Annica

And the family of God: all those who have been the Body of Christ to me, especially those who have helped and encouraged me in the production of Spirit Dance.

Acknowledgement

I acknowledge my mother,
Adah Irene Wright Cross,
as my first, and even now unsurpassed, example
of what it means to be a Christian.
Because of her love for Jesus, compassion for people,
and creativity with words,
I hope this work will honor her.

Preface

Do you long to escape a dry Christianity and find a vibrant all-consuming faith in Jesus that defines and directs you? Then maybe the Holy Spirit has something specific for you somewhere in the pages of *Spirit Dance*. The purpose of this preface is to introduce some poetry that contains glimpses of the intensity and importance of the teaching in this book. Because of its symbolic nature, this poetry is not easily understood except in the context of the whole teaching.

So, for now, let it be like a few brightly colored puzzle pieces that can only suggest the finished picture. Just as a movie preview flashes a few images to create a collage of impressions that make you want to experience the whole movie, perhaps some bits of these verses will spark interest in *Spirit Dance*.

The poem is a very subjective, gut-level expression of many of the spiritual concepts presented in this book. As you will see, the book itself is mostly straight forward, logical teaching with occasional flurries of passion and gusts of incongruous humor.

As the teaching in *Spirit Dance* unfolds, the stanzas of the *Escape of an Intellectual* poem will appear again individually where appropriate throughout the text. However, I wanted the poem in its entirety somewhere. So here it is, where it is intended only to be scanned before one reads the book, but it will be in a convenient place for future reference.

The first chapter of this book will focus on introducing the spirit dance teaching. As you will see, spirit dance represents an ideal pattern of growth in Christ. However, as we find our way from Old Covenant to New Covenant thinking, there are inevitable deceptions and confusions along the way.

The poem speaks of those detours in our journey, which are different for all of us and yet contain common threads. Christians go through patterns of departure and return. Whether we learn quickly or slowly, with difficulty or ease, making progress usually involves some type of coming full circle to define and own what we believe.

Our understanding of the process of spiritual growth can either limit or enhance our experience with that process. At the same time, what we actually experience as we go through that process is what makes our beliefs unquestionably ours.

The main question to the believer who is just starting to read this book is: Do you want to make your relationship with Jesus stronger, clearer, and more exciting and productive than ever before? If so, you will find *Spirit Dance* well worth reading.

Don't get bogged down with the *Escape of an Intellectual* poem at this point. Just scan it and recognize in a general way the spiritual journey it reflects. Notice the five Ds—one for each stanza. **Doubting** leads to **distancing** ourselves from God. After distancing come spiritual **drought**, then **despair**. Finally we come to the possibility of a new intimacy symbolized in the **dance**.

These two, the *Escape of an Intellectual* poem and the whole spirit dance teaching, when taught together, make a powerful case for grace. Understanding grace is the secret of success for Christians. Our enemy (Satan) has tried to distort our view of grace in order to stunt our growth.

Christians are being called to rise up out of our insecurity and fulfill our place in history with courage and passion. For some of us, the next step is to run past our theology into the arms of God.

ESCAPE OF AN INTELLECTUAL
(or *A Frolic Past Theology into the Arms of God*)
© by Margaret Westphal

Ambiguous analysis
leads from the spirit to the mind,
where faith drifts beside deception
and disappointment starts to grind
against simplicity,
now turned inside out,
dimmed by nagging doubt,
and diluted along the way
by a sad, sophisticated
            shade of gray.

Numb resignation
masquerades as grace.
Insecurity calls itself submission
in this passive polluted place.
Taunted by fear and unbelief,
hopelessness offers a false relief,
but distorts Your voice and blurs Your face.
You look foreboding, undefined, and far away
through my safe, self-sufficient
            shield of gray.

Lonely legalism
looks so right but feels so empty.
I'm tired and dry—Your strength has left me.
There's no life in my efforts or truth in my trying
to die to myself when I'm really just dying.
But Christ in me could fulfill my call
with no shadow of turning, no darkness at all.
The web of deception is starting to fray.
The fire of my first love is
                melting the gray.

Homesick heartache
to contain Your zeal again—
but my stiff cold wineskin
has no capacity for Your fire,
and my religious sensibility
scoffs at my desire
to leap into Your love and stay
where Your purity defines me
and Your faith flows
                  free from gray.

Passionate innocence—
Your Spirit dancing with mine,
saturates and softens
my wineskin with Your wine.
Jesus, You fill me with effortless trust
and I'm splashing in Your laughter
that washes me away
to Your peace beyond my pain
and into Your glory
                past the gray.

Contents

Introduction

As one who came to know Christ in childhood, I've always found it fascinating to explore the subject of how we as believers relate to God. As I have raised my children, I've wondered how God raises His children. We seem pretty dysfunctional when compared to the New Testament church.

Early Christians had more supernatural power evident in answer to their prayers for healing, protection, direction, etc. That's not the only contrast we see between now and then. What about changed lives? Why do American Christians suffer from so many of the same moral failures and personality quirks as non-Christians?

Some say that the church is not strong because our society has become so immoral. But we, the church, are to be a light for the world's darkness. If the world is not coming to the church's light, it is because they don't see the brightness of His glory in us.

For the last twenty years I've heard prophecies of great revival coming to the American church. When that happens we will not only see many more miracles, but we will also see many more Christians whose lives really do reflect the character of Jesus.

How will all this happen? Are we just waiting on God or is He somehow waiting on us? Instinctively we know that the security and significance we long for is to be found in our relationship with Jesus.

The problem is that to many Christians, Jesus seems unreachable, almost unreal. For this reason, many have drifted into hedonism (if it feels good do it), or else they have turned to religion and the idea that doing enough good works will lead to finding peace with God and themselves. These are both ultimately painful, dead-end roads.

It's so easy to lose our way or stay stuck in the same rut. This book is for those who want to re-examine the process of how Jesus actually transforms us. Some call this process sanctification, holiness, or spiritual formation. Understanding how this process works is vital, not just for our growth but to enable us to accomplish what we were created to do.

As we try to understand the truth about the process, we will discover that the truth is not so much what to believe but who. The truth is a Person. Jesus said that He is the way, the truth, and the life. He did not say that He is the way director, the truth teller, and the life example. To say that would not have been wrong, just very limited. He didn't just come to bring us a set of ideas or instructions. He brought us Himself. Christianity is not a lifestyle. It is a life form. It's not a doctrine—it's a dance!

I submit this work as a prophetic call of the Bridegroom (Jesus) to the bride (the church). It is also the prayer of the bride to the Bridegroom. We know that there is something beyond our Laodicean fog, our impotent churchiness. The Holy Spirit cries out, both on our behalf for more of Him and on His behalf for more of us. Whether you hear that cry as a faint ache or a passionate roar, it is still deep calling to deep (Psalms 42:7).

We're all learning and growing as we experience more of Him. For years, every time I thought I understood grace, the Holy Spirit showed me even more. I'm sure I'm still on the edges of grasping the wonder of it all, but I feel compelled to communicate what took the Lord years—several decades actually—to teach me.

May the following pages draw you closer to Jesus, the One full of grace and truth. This book is not for the satisfied believer who doesn't want his doctrinal boat rocked. The following chapters are meant to challenge both head and heart as you venture out on a wild ride into pure, free, passionate, in-your-face *grace*.

One

The Call to Escape

Christians, like people in general, tend to be either more analytical or more intuitive. We all have heads and hearts, but with some of us you reach our heart through our head, and with others you reach our head through our heart. This natural leaning, along with our theological background and personal experiences, makes each of us relate to God either more experientially or more intellectually.

Blockheads and airheads

Are you more of a thinker or a feeler? Are you more drawn to the natural or the supernatural, the Word of God or the moving of the Holy Spirit? These camps have sadly, at times, chosen up sides, called each other names, and turned the world off to Jesus.

People of either inclination can become spiritually strong. In the Bible, we see Paul and James as more analytical types and Peter and John as probably more intuitive. All became great men of God.

We are all created to be different but all in the image of God. When we're abiding in Christ, each of us reflects part of Jesus' character and call. Jesus said, "He that hath seen me hath seen the Father" (John 14:9 KJV). We should be able to say, "If you've seen us (the whole body of Christ) you've seen Jesus."

The analyticals can become dry and legalistic, and see the intuitives as weird, superficial airheads. In defense of the analyticals, the Bible does say we are to "renew our minds" (Romans 12:2). So we know that we are not to throw out intellectual integrity as we grow in Christ. In defense of the intuitives, there will always be a mysterious, subjective aspect to our relationship with God. The created cannot fully understand the Creator. Knowledge can lead to pride (1 Corinthians 8:1). The pride of thinking we know all about God can be a spiritual block.

> **Trust in the Lord with all thine heart; and lean not unto thine own understanding.**
>
> **Proverbs 3:5 KJV**

Actually, few people would fall in these extreme categories of blockheads or airheads. Balance is defined by however we are, right? Personally, I'm something of a recovering intellectual.

Is God too deep to understand? Is He too far away to be experienced? Let's look at some scripture. **Romans 11:33–34** says,

> **Oh, the depth of the riches and wisdom and knowledge of God! How unfathomable (inscrutable, unsearchable) are His judgments (His decisions)! And how untraceable (mysterious, undiscoverable) are His ways (His methods, His paths)!**
>
> **For who has known the mind of the Lord *and* who has understood His thoughts, or who has [ever] been His counselor?**

Romans 12:2 says,

> **Do not be conformed to this world (this age), [fashioned after and adapted to its external, superficial customs], but be trans-**

formed (changed) by the [entire] renewal of your mind [by its new ideals and its new attitude], so that you may prove [for yourselves] what is the good and acceptable and perfect will of God, even the thing which is good and acceptable and perfect [in His sight for you].

How do we get from the way-too-deep God to the One who supernaturally transforms us and reveals to us His will for our lives? Back up to **Romans 12:1** which says,

I appeal to you therefore, brethren, and beg of you in view of [all] the mercies of God, to make a decisive dedication of your bodies [presenting all your members and faculties] as a living sacrifice, holy (devoted, consecrated) and well pleasing to God, which is your reasonable (rational, intelligent) service and spiritual worship.

This verse speaks of an ongoing, interactive process of presenting ourselves to God. It is called both "reasonable" and "spiritual" in this scripture. This book is a study of that process. For the intellectual it could be called *the upward spiral of spiritual growth*. And for the intuitive—*spirit dance*.

How did I get in this desert?

Many Christians (including both airhead and blockhead types) find themselves desperately dry, or at best bored, in their relationships with the Lord. Many never intentionally left their first love but find themselves feeling far from the presence and power of God. Perhaps because there was no conscious distancing, they don't know what happened or how to get back to the excitement, mystery, and adventure that should be a part of knowing and serving Jesus.

Lukewarm may be common, but it isn't normal!

When I cried out in my wilderness season, "How did I get here and how can I get back," the Lord gave me a poem called *Escape of an Intellectual.* The spirit dance process represents an ideal pattern of continuous growth. Of course, we don't always make progress ideally or continuously. This poem shows some of our common struggles. Stanzas of *Escape of an Intellectual* will appear individually throughout the book as the various concepts are addressed. All five stanzas of the poem are together at the end of the preface to this book.

The goal of this first chapter is to explain the basic flow of the dance, as illustrated in the diagram below. Subsequent chapters will deal with biblical analysis of each of the steps. **John 1:14** KJV says,

> **And the Word was made flesh, and dwelt among us, (and we beheld his glory, the glory as of the only begotten of the Father,) full of grace and truth.**

My prayer is that as you read this, Jesus will, by the Holy Spirit, dwell with you and you will behold more of His glory, grace, and truth.

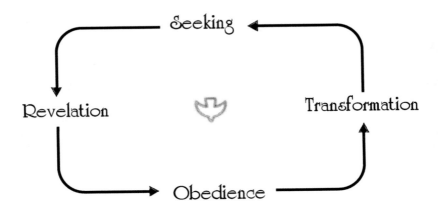

Introduction of the dance

The preceding illustration is the basic concept that will serve as a foundation for all the rest of the teachings in this book. Spirit dance is not some new theological revelation. It is a simple way to understand and articulate the interactive process that happens in our ongoing relationship with Jesus.

The better we understand the process, the more we can consistently cooperate with it in faith. It is important to understand what we are experiencing *and* to experience what we understand. We need to solidify our foundation. What do we really believe and how can we live it? Our security and significance are only found in Him.

This diagram illustrates the spirit dance teaching. The **seeking** and **obedience** are our parts—what we do (with His power, of course). The **revelation** and **transformation** are what God does toward us. If we **seek**, we find. Find what? Further **revelation** about Jesus. That **revelation** will call for a response from us. When we respond, that **obedience** allows God to **transform** us. Being changed, we are then empowered to continue **seeking** with a purer heart and a greater passion than before.

In a dance, two move as one; but one is leading, and the other is following. Our relationship with the Lord is an even more intimate process than the dance analogy suggests. We are not just following His lead, as in doing a Jesus imitation. He is not just showing us what to do. He is actually doing it through us. Paul said, "Christ in you, the hope of glory" (Colossians 1:27 KJV).

Even the parts of the dance that we think are our own actions are empowered by Him. We **seek** because He draws us. We **obey** because He enables us. And yet we never lose our free will. Our participation is continually required—thus the dance! It's a dance toward wholeness, toward more in-*Him*-ness.

It's more an art than a science, but there's much to understand. Approach this book as a way to shine some scriptural light on your own adventure with Jesus. Whether you've known Him for decades or days, looking at these phases of the dance and struggles in the poem may help you see more clearly where you are, where you've been, and where you can be.

Let's start with the **seeking**. Why seek? What is seeking? What happens when seeking gets off track? In upcoming chapters we'll look at these things. We'll also examine the desert experience that was mentioned before and what happens when we mess up in life and/or life messes us up.

Looking at times of brokenness and what happens in the spiritual battleground of the heart brings up some of the oldest, hardest, and most fascinating questions. I certainly don't have all the answers, but I bet I can make you think—and feel!

Two

Battleground
of the Broken Heart

O God, you are my God, earnestly will I seek You; my inner self thirsts for You, my flesh longs *and* is faint for You, in a dry and weary land where no water is.

Psalms 63:1

an you identify with the desert experience that David describes in this Psalm? Spiritual dryness is a call to **seek** God. If you are dry you're blessed because at least you know you are off track. The truly lukewarm don't know. They are busy "having a form of godliness but denying the power thereof" (2 Timothy 3:5 KJV). They think they are "in need of nothing" (Revelation 3:17). The Bridegroom is calling the bride of Christ back into the dance, back to intimacy and power. So if you hear that call, you are blessed.

Some of you have bottomed out before, perhaps many times. Each time you vowed to start over and try harder only to find yourself failing again, giving up for a while, and then going back into another cycle of rededication. Going through continuous cycles of rededication is a symptom of living under law instead of grace, self-sufficiency instead of abiding in the vine, flesh instead of spirit, works instead of faith. All these phrases have to do with Old Covenant versus New Covenant concepts.

We first get off track in the **seeking** stage. When Christians go through times of brokenness (translation: life happens and it hurts) our hearts become a spiritual battleground. Unanswered questions lead to doubt. Subtle deception creeps in that challenges God's integrity, and our original childlike faith becomes muddled, gray, lukewarm.

This disillusionment is often reinforced by religious teaching. Since we sense this same sadness in fellow Christians, we begin to assume that it is inevitable. This state is described in the first stanza of *Escape of an Intellectual*.

> Ambiguous analysis
> leads from the spirit to the mind,
> where faith drifts beside deception
> and disappointment starts to grind
> against simplicity,
> now turned inside out,
> dimmed by nagging doubt,
> and diluted along the way
> by a sad, sophisticated
> shade of gray.

In this disoriented state of brokenness, we are very vulnerable. We become like a "house divided against itself" (Mark 3:25) or a "double-minded man" (James 1:8 KJV).

During this time, **God wants us to find wholeness in Him and lay down self-sufficiency. But Satan wants us to harden our hearts with self-sufficiency and question God's integrity.**

Read these last two sentences again. These are the two possible outcomes in a time of spiritual crises and disorientation in the life of a Christian. It is possible, even common, to have the second reaction and think we're having the first. It's called religion. This wrong reaction is very subtle because it looks like the real thing. But something is a little twisted.

The older brother in the prodigal son story didn't appear to have a problem until circumstances revealed a deep-seated insecurity in his perception of his father. On the outside, this older brother had been working hard and doing everything right. On the inside, though, he had left home too. He had left his position of pure-hearted devotion and trust in relation to his father.

He had come to question his father's integrity and see him as a withholder. He had the same problem that his prodigal brother had—wrong father image. They both ran away in their own way. One ran in rebellion and the other in works (like religion). Both had the same root problem—bad father image.

Jesus told us this parable because He knew we all would be tempted to run, either as a prodigal or as an older brother. I can't say that I fully understand the prodigals since I've not had a season of outward rebellion, but I have particular compassion for the older brother who runs on the inside. I have been him.

Paul was concerned about the early Christians becoming spiritually disoriented. **2 Corinthians 11:3** says,

> But [now] I am fearful, lest that even as the serpent beguiled Eve by his cunning, so your minds may be corrupted *and* seduced from wholehearted *and* sincere *and* pure devotion to Christ.

Many in the body of Christ today have been seduced from wholehearted devotion to Jesus. The devil's prime way to seduce us is to get us to question our revelation of the goodness and integrity of our God. The line he used with Eve is still one of his most effective. "Hath God said…?" (Genesis 3:1) or in other words, "Maybe God's not quite as good as you think."

The devil was not dumb enough to say to Eve, "Why don't you rebel against God?" He just planted a seed of doubt. Likewise, in dealing with us, the devil doesn't say, "Why don't you backslide and ruin your life and the lives of those you love?" No, just a seed of doubt is presented, "Maybe this whole Christianity thing is not exactly what you thought."

Doubt will come. Sometimes it is a subtle seed, an idea slipped into the mind like poison in our food that gradually makes us sick. Other times there's no subtlety to it. Doubt and unbelief can explode like a terrorist's bomb ripping us apart.

No more melodies

For me the bomb dropped when I was fourteen years old. My ten-year-old brother had gone to the hospital with a ruptured appendix. After his operation he had remained in the hospital where we visited him each day for the next few days. As I went about my daily school routine that week, I constantly prayed for my brother, making up little melodies in my heart, songs sung to God in my childlike faith.

And then one night at my grandmother's house, my sister and I woke up to a terrifying sound. All the adults who should have been at the hospital were in the other room crying, men and women both. With my brother's death, a dark curtain fell on my childhood.

People tried to comfort us with talk about God's will. I found nothing comforting in that. Their kind but ignorant answers to my questions led me to conclude that adults don't know much about God either. I remember asking someone why we pray at all if God's will is going to happen anyway. They said it makes us feel better. I thought to myself, *well if it makes you feel better, carry on, but I don't have any need to communicate with a child-killing God.*

It was as if God had taken a hostage and if I ever wanted to see my brother again I would have to be careful to earn that privilege by living by God's rules. At the funeral, someone said to me, "There will be a reunion." I clung to that hope thinking that maybe a God who plans a reunion is not all bad.

But my Christianity became little more than hell insurance, a business deal with a God I didn't like much anymore. They say time heals all wounds. That's not true. Jesus is the healer but not until we allow Him to be. I put up tough walls. No more childlike melodies.

God would have to wait years for a little crack of faith in my wall of works. He wanted to bring **revelation** and **transformation** to me, but I had quit **seeking.**

> But without faith *it is* impossible to please *him:* for he that cometh to God must believe that he is, and *that* he is a rewarder of them that diligently seek him.
>
> Hebrews 11:6 KJV

Three

Discovering Identity

For as he thinks in his heart, so is he.

Proverbs 23:7

Since this battle for our heart is so important, let's consider how to define the heart. There's been a lot of teaching about the definitions of spirit, soul, and body. Not everyone agrees on definitions for these, much less how the heart fits into the whole being.

The body is the most obvious part of us. I've heard it called our earth suit. Essential as it is to function on this planet, it is only our outer shell. I believe the spirit to be the real us. When we accept Christ, our spirit becomes alive to God. It was already alive before but not alive to God. Some call it getting saved, experiencing regeneration, or becoming a new creature in Christ. Whatever your terminology, the Holy Spirit comes into our spirit and brings the nature of life and light and righteousness in place of the nature of sin and death that was in our spirit.

This great exchange, accomplished at Calvary and appropriated by our decision, is the exchange of our sin for His righteousness. He became sin for us even though He didn't commit sin; we became His righteousness even though we did not commit righteousness. When we became a new creature in Christ (2 Corinthians 5:7), our spirit (the real us) became totally righteous because His righteousness was imputed to us. That means we're completely fixed! If we're saved, we are as accepted and loved by God right now as we will ever be.

So why aren't Christians behaving perfectly from the time they get saved? There is a transformation process that must take place in the soul. The soul is the part of us that is in the process of getting fixed. Our soul includes our mind, our will, and our emotions. Think of it as the personality package. The process of sanctification changes us from the inside out as the grace (enabling power) of God in our spirit changes our soul (mind, will, and emotions).

What is the heart?

So what is the heart? Some say it's the same thing as the spirit. Others say it's another word for the soul. There are hundreds of references to the heart in scripture. Some sound like they could mean the spirit, and some sound like the soul.

I was unsure how to define the heart until I read Dr. James Richards' definition in his book *Grace: the Power to Change.* He says,

The heart is the place where who you are in your spirit and who you are in your soul come together.[1]

This makes a lot of sense. No wonder Satan wants to mess with our hearts. If our heart is the connection between our spirit and our soul, then to interfere at this level messes with our very identity.

Our spirit, the real, already-righteous us, is in touch with the Holy Spirit at all times. Our soul, being still under construction, needs constant direction from our spirit. If our heart condition cuts us off from that guidance of the Holy Spirit in our spirit, then we are in trouble. We can get disconnected from our life source and who we really are.

> **Keep *and* guard your heart with all vigilance *and* above all that you guard, for out of it flow the springs of life.**
>
> Proverbs 4:23

How do we keep our hearts? We must guard that connection between the real us in our spirit and our soul that is in the process of being fixed. We must continually identify with—see ourselves as being—the new creature we are. Our heart must stay open and willing to trust a God who is ready to flow through our born-again spirit and empower our soul. Our soul is our under-construction personality that has to change when our spirit takes charge.

You will progressively become who you see yourself as being. Satan's only tools are deception and accusation. He cannot change the truth, only our perception of it.

When life presents unanswered questions, Satan jumps in to attack our image of God and also our image of who we are in Christ. Consider this quote by Mike Bickle from his book *The Pleasures of Loving God:*

Satan attacks us by undermining our revelation of God. When we lose the revelation of Him as our Bridegroom, we forget His tenderness, His embrace and His kindness to us. Then we do not feel cherished by Him in our weakness, we begin to be distracted from pure devotion.[2]

Similarly, Dr. James Richards says,

Tribulation does not come to develop or help you; it comes to destroy you. Your response to tribulation is what determines its effect. When going through difficult times, it is essential that the heart remain stable and steadfast in truth. When the heart begins to waiver, to the same degree that your emotions begin to change, you will hinder grace from flowing out of you. Once you stop the flow of grace, you are limited to the extent of your own ability.[3]

Most Christians understand that salvation is received by grace through faith (Ephesians 2:8). But many have no concept of sanctification as coming by grace through faith also. They start out God-powered and end up manpowered.

If the devil can't keep us from getting saved, his next plan is to keep us miserable, unproductive, and making no progress in Christ. How does he do it? He does it by keeping us stuck in the Old Covenant.

The spirit of the Old Covenant

When Moses gave the law to the Israelites, their reply reflects the spirit of the Old Covenant. They said, "All that the Lord hath said will we do and be obedient" (Exodus 24:7). They thought that if they just knew what to do they could do it. Were they sincere? Yes. But the next thousand years proved that they could not keep the law. There was nothing wrong with the Old Covenant except man's inability to keep it.

Andrew Murray in his book *The Two Covenants* does a magnificent job of showing how the Old and New Covenants in history parallel Old Covenant and New Covenant stages in the life of the believer. As I meditated in this little book for a couple of years recently, God used it to soak a few more layers of legalism off me. The central theme of *The Two Covenants* is that in the Old Covenant man could not keep his part of the covenant with God. But in the New Covenant, God undertakes to do both His part **and** our part through us.

The devil would like to keep us forever stuck in the Old Covenant, forever trying to serve God in our own strength, and forever struggling. Dr. James Richards says,

Probably the greatest frustration among serious believers is the inability to change. For the most part, Christians seem to keep their problems for a lifetime.[4]

Yet **Romans 6:14** tells us,

For sin shall not [any longer] exert dominion over you, since now you are not under Law [as slaves], but under grace [as subjects of God's favor and mercy].

The truth is that we get saved by grace and then try to continue on in our own ability to keep the law. Having believed our way into salvation, we then begin working our way to holiness.

Are you so foolish *and* so senseless *and* so silly? Having begun [your new life spiritually] with the [Holy} Spirit, are you now reaching perfection [by dependence] on the flesh?
Galatians 3:3

This whole law and grace thing seems confusing until it suddenly becomes obvious. The lesson of the Old Covenant is "we can't do it." Getting past self-sufficiency doesn't come easily. But at the end of us, we find the beginning of Jesus!

It's going to be either His power or ours. It's law or grace, works or faith, our efforts or His. We can't have it both ways. Either we get out of His way and let Him be all through us, or He gets out of our way and lets us keep on trying to do it on our own.

There is a battle for your heart, and that battle is for your spiritual identity. We were designed to be white hot and wholehearted for God. We are to be wholehearted in two respects—not only spiritually strong in our relationship with God, but as a result of that relationship, wholeheartedly giving ourselves with total abandonment to do all that He calls us to do. The bride of Christ will rise up in these last days in the power of *His* might—not ours.

> **Finally, my brethren, be strong in the Lord, and in the power of his might.**
>
> Ephesians 6:10 KJV

We knew we had nothing to contribute to our salvation. We just jumped in and trusted Him for the whole thing. Why can't we do the same thing for sanctification? It takes a supernatural revelation of grace. Seek that revelation.

> **And ye shall seek *me*, and find me, when ye shall search for me with all your heart.**
>
> Jeremiah 29:13 KJV

As a young Christian I knew little about seeking God. I was a law keeper. As a born-again believer I understood the importance of accepting Jesus' sacrifice for our sin; but then, beyond that decision, I felt it was up to the believer to know the Bible and follow the rules. I remember thinking once when I was a teenager that the whole matter would be a lot simpler if I were Jewish. Then all I'd have to do is know the rules and follow them. I could have handled that, I thought, but I was never quite sure what Jesus required of me beyond a salvation decision.

I sought to obey God without seeking Him personally. There were many happy things going on in my life, especially marrying my high school sweetheart when we were both twenty-one and finishing our last few semesters of college. An unexpected spiritual breakthrough came not too long after we were married.

A time of seeking

After receiving word that a friend had just lost her brother in an accident, I sat down to write her a note and collapsed into tears.

What could I write to my friend? I knew nothing helpful about losing a brother because my nightmare had never really ended. I had gone on with my life while the grief went underground. It was like somewhere on the inside I had never quit crying. I was shocked to realize that buried under all my busyness and good works there was still a frightened, angry fourteen-year-old.

In fact, I had become worse because my grief had grown tentacles of unbelief. The unbelief had become a greater problem than the original grief. The depth of that unbelief was startling to face.

I found myself praying about all of this for the first time. I said, "God, I'm no better than I was years ago right after my brother died. Something in me is terribly broken and I'll never be able to fix myself. I'll always be messed up unless You do something. I think I could stand it if I really knew my brother was all right. But to be honest I don't know that heaven is not just something men made up to try to stay sane. I don't even know anymore if You're real, God. For all I know I'm talking to the wall right now."

I went on asking for some kind of help and then stared around the silent room feeling silly. "Well, that was really dumb," I told myself, "God is probably real but He's certainly not obligated to prove anything to anybody. Faith is a blind thing. I don't know what I was expecting anyway." I dropped the matter, but Someone heard—Someone who had been waiting a long time.

The vision

A few nights later while I was asleep, I was taken somewhere. My physical body never left the bed that night; but nevertheless, I was suddenly somewhere alone. There was no visible scenery around me, not even under me. A voice from behind me called my name and I turned around to find myself face to face with my brother who had died. He was taller, older, but it was unquestionably him.

I have never been happier than I was there, laughing and crying in his arms. We communicated much without words. It was like we could each read the other's thoughts. Only a few words were spoken.

I said, "You don't know how many times I've wished that I could know that you are all right."

"Yes, I do know," he responded.

Then later I said, "This all seems as real as anything I've ever experienced, but it's not possible for me to see you. So I must be dreaming."

He smiled and told me firmly, "No, you're not dreaming."

I was then drawn slowly back to being awake in my bed. There were no good-byes, just instructions from somewhere telling me not to forget the experience as I was being brought back. It was morning, and I got up but couldn't speak at first. My husband asked if I was all right. I said, "I don't think I've ever been more all right."

Concerning unbelief

I hesitate to share this experience because I can't explain it. All I know is that it was a gift of grace. The Lord gave me this revelation of the coming reunion as an answer to prayer.[5]

Was it a dream or not? There are many different kinds of dreams. Some have no spiritual significance and others do. The reason I believe the experience was something other than an ordinary dream (or any kind of dream) is because it had to be in order to cut through my level of unbelief at the time. Had I not been told specifically that this experience was not really a dream, my unbelief would probably have later diluted the experience into being perceived as only a product of my imagination or the wishful thinking of a troubled mind.

Remember the scripture about an angel coming to Joseph in a dream to tell him to believe Mary's story about her conception and go ahead with plans to marry her? Did an angel really come to him or did Joseph just dream that he saw an angel? The important thing, of course, is that he got the message. However, Joseph was dealing with unbelief. Apparently God will go to extreme measures to deal with honest unbelief.

Honest unbelief is unbelief that wants to believe. This is quite different than the kind of unbelief that is an excuse for rebellion. This issue of unbelief will be further addressed in later chapters of this book.

I cannot say that after this supernatural deliverance from some of my unbelief, I then began to grow spiritually by leaps and bounds. I wasn't seeking consistently. I had no idea how. But I finally knew that God was 100% good and that He loved me so much that He would even temporarily rearrange time and space to minister to me. I was no longer afraid of Him or mad at Him.

I still had a lot to learn and unlearn, but the dance was underway. I was still very much a legalist, but I'd seen a glimpse of grace. The Lord of the dance would eventually lead me out of the spirit of the Old Covenant.

> Blessed *are* they which do hunger and thirst after righteousness: for they shall be filled.
>
> Matthew 5:6 KJV

Four

Counterfeit Wholeness

S elf-sufficiency is counterfeit wholeness. Doubting leads us, consciously or unconsciously, to distance ourselves from God. Distancing is expressed through rebellion or religion; both of which are expressions of the flesh.

Having lost our first love, being tricked into disconnection from our source, we run like Adam and Eve to hide in the bushes of rebellion and not relate to God. Or, we come out of the bushes of rebellion covered fig-leaf style (portable mini bush) ready to deal with God religiously. But we feel like hypocrites because we are. Our performance is just that—a performance. We long to be real.

Read the next two stanzas of *Escape of an Intellectual.* These stanzas deal with the pain of distancing ourselves from God and the futility of trying to find our way back by works. They basically say that giving up doesn't help and neither does trying harder. So how are we going to escape? Jesus already came to bust us out!

Numb resignation
masquerades as grace.
Insecurity calls itself submission
in this passive polluted place.
Taunted by fear and unbelief,
hopelessness offers a false relief,
but distorts your voice and blurs your face.
You look foreboding, undefined, and far away
through my safe, self-sufficient
                              shield of gray.

Lonely legalism
looks so right but feels so empty.
I'm tired and dry—your strength has left me.
There's no life in my efforts or truth in my trying
to die to myself when I'm really just dying.
But Christ in me could fulfill my call
with no shadow of turning, no darkness at all.
The web of deception is starting to fray.
The fire of my first love is
                              melting the gray.

The road and the ditches

These extremes of giving up and trying harder in our own strength are like ditches that we fall into as we try to go down the road of being led and empowered by the Holy Spirit. I found that if I continually overcorrected myself, I would just change ditches instead of making progress in my relationship with the Lord.

For instance, if I got discouraged and gave up on my prayer and Bible reading, I would then after a while be so disappointed with myself that I would set ridiculously unrealistic goals in these disciplines. Then when I couldn't keep up, I'd get discouraged again and not do anything. The Lord couldn't help me travel down the road because He couldn't catch me as I blundered past Him on my way back and forth from ditch to ditch.

The Lord reminded me of how I learned to ride a bicycle. There was a dirt driveway that went down a little hill by our house on the farm. When learning to ride, we would take off on our bike from the top of the hill. It took a lot of courage the first few times because we knew that one of three things could happen. We could fall over to the right, or we could fall over to the left, or maybe, if we were lucky, we would get the feel of it and stay balanced. We knew that sooner or later we would discover how to stay upright all the way down and avoid the agony of defeat.

The Lord showed me that these ditches of quitting and trying too hard (relying on our own strength) are spiritual accidents. He knows that some crashing off to one extreme and the other will happen in our attempt to get the feel of being led by the Spirit. The trick is, when we realize we're in a ditch, we need to get out without going over and falling off the other side.

Getting free

Maybe, if you've never thought outside the realm of performance-based religion, this all sounds really foreign. We are so used to thinking in terms of what we must *do*. The preaching of grace is sometimes misinterpreted as *sloppy agape*, as if it's risky to let people feel too secure.

Paul preached freedom in Christ and called himself a love slave, one who serves out of "want to" and "get to" instead of "have to." You'll do a thousand times more for love than you ever did for duty. Perfect love casts out fear (1 John 4:18). Fear paralyzes. Faith energizes.

The bride of Christ—an abused wife?

An abused wife is one without security. She may love her husband and be dependent on him, but she dares not trust him. After all, she never knows for sure if she is about to get blessed or hurt.

Many Christians see God that way. They are as committed as one can be to a God that may suddenly, at any time, smack them with a good dose of cancer, bankruptcy, car wrecks, or earthquakes. They may console themselves with the thought that whatever pain comes is mysteriously for their own good and is some sort of blessing in disguise. But secretly they hope He "blesses" someone else. Self-sufficiency seems safer than trusting God.

One time, as a young wife and mother, I asked my husband a preposterous question. I had heard of several cases of adultery by husbands I would never have suspected. I knew I wasn't the best wife in the world, especially in the areas of house cleaning and child discipline.

So, wondering how much security I really had in Russell, I said to him, "I'm going to ask you a question that's going to sound funny, but please don't laugh at me because I'm very serious and I really want to know. What if I gained a hundred pounds and I never lost it, and I never got the house clean again, and never cooked another decent meal, and I completely lost control of the kids, and never said another pleasant word? Would you still always love me, stay with me, be faithful to me, and try to help me?" He looked at me kindly and said yes, never cracking a smile.

Isn't that amazing? What's even more amazing is that I believed him. Was it risky for him to reveal such unconditional love? Would I then be tempted to take advantage of it? Of course not! And the Lord spoke in my spirit later and said, "That's how I love my bride, too."

The bride of Christ, the church, is so concerned about all her spots and wrinkles, so worried about all her weaknesses. She needs to see her Bridegroom. She would no longer have such problems with trust and obedience if she ever really saw Him.

No wonder Satan doesn't want us to see the Bridegroom clearly. If we did, we'd fall crazy in love with Him and knowing Him would become the all-consuming passion of our lives. Paul considered everything else in his life in the dung category when compared to "knowing Him" (Philippians 3:8 KJV).

Knowing Him more and more

Knowing Him happens progressively. Some parts of the dance that we go through are calm and ordinary and some are down right dramatic. There was a time in my earlier years of getting to know Jesus that I came to realize that I must be missing something, but I didn't know what it was.

It would annoy me when I'd hear people talk about Jesus in a passionate, personal way. I would think, *Oh, get real, it's not that emotional or intimate, you are just getting carried away or trying to look extra spiritual.* I developed my own little Pharisee theory that all these people fell into one of two categories. Either they were emotionally unstable like children who go around talking to an imaginary friend or else they were cons who just wanted to impress or manipulate people with their religious superiority. I diagnosed them as either weak or fake.

But, after a while, I began to meet people who talked about Jesus in a very personal way and yet they wouldn't fit in either of my categories. They were just strong, stable, honest Christians who seemed to be in touch with Jesus in some way that I wasn't.

One of these people who wouldn't fit in my categories was a close friend so I decided to come right out and ask her about it. I said, "I have no doubts about my salvation and I really love the Lord just like you do, but why is it that you seem to get so much more strength and joy from your relationship with God than I do? I know that He loves me, but He seems so far away and I feel like I'm so on my own and get stressed out so easily. You have harder situations in your life than I do, and yet you're nearly always happy. What's wrong with me?"

She said, "There's nothing wrong with you. You just need the Holy Spirit. I've got some books that you can read about the baptism of the Holy Spirit. Take them home and let me know what you think." I had no idea what she was talking about, but I went home and studied it out. As I read, I got more and more excited. When I became convinced that this was what I was looking for, I prayed and stepped into a new supernatural level of the dance.

Paul's dance

Talk about dramatic! The apostle Paul's first encounter with the Lord of the dance looked more like kung fu. Paul got a shocking revelation of Jesus. Before that, Paul thought he was **obeying** God, but in reality he was obeying a **revelation** that was not at all from God. Paul had not been doing well in the **seeking** part of the dance, so Jesus resorted to the ready-or-not-here-I-come approach. On the Damascus Road, Paul was struck down by a real **revelation** of God. He then **obeyed** a series of instructions to go to a certain place and receive prayer from a certain person.

His **revelation** and subsequent **obedience** resulted in a supernatural **transformation** when he recovered his sight and was filled with the Holy Spirit. He continued **seeking** and **obeying** God from then on and God continued **revealing** things to Paul and **transforming** His "chosen instrument" from glory to glory.

And all of us, as with unveiled face, [because we] continued to behold [in the Word of God] as in a mirror the glory of the Lord, are constantly being transfigured into His *very own* image in ever increasing splendor *and* from one degree of glory to another; [for this comes] from the Lord [Who is] the Spirit.

2 Corinthians 3:18

Paul was used mightily by God; but his focus, his driving force, was not to do for God but to "know Him."

[For my determined purpose is] that I may know Him [that I may progressively become more deeply and intimately acquainted with Him, perceiving and recognizing and understanding the wonders of His Person more strongly and more clearly].

Philippians 3:10

Knowing Him results in doing for Him, not the other way around. **Revelation** calls for **obedience**. To see Him is to love Him, and to love Him is to serve Him.

Five

River—Desert—Ministry

aul's revelation of the grace of God and what it means to be in Christ has inspired generations. Paul walked in power and humility; he knew who he was and who he wasn't. Knowing who we aren't does not mean having a low opinion of ourselves. It means having an accurate perception of ourselves.

Jesus certainly did not have a low opinion of himself, but He walked in total humility. Andrew Murray wrote, "The deepest secret of Jesus' life on earth was His dependence on the Father."[6] Murray points out how Jesus used the words "not" and "nothing" about himself many times in scripture. Jesus used phrases like **not** my words, **not** my will, **not** my honor, **not** mine own glory. He said things like, "I can do **nothing** of myself. I speak **not** of myself. I came **not** of myself. I do **nothing** of myself."

Jesus lived in childlike dependence and allowed the Father to do everything through Him. He knew who He was and who He wasn't.

He was on a mission, but He was not doing His own thing. He was not acting by His own authority.

But didn't He have authority? Wasn't He God? Didn't He know it? Certainly. Many scriptures speak of His divinity.

> **Before Abraham was, I am.**   John 8:58 KJV
>
> **Anyone who has seen Me has seen the Father.**   John 14:9
>
> **I and the Father are One.**   John 10:30
>
> **All authority (all power of rule) in heaven and on earth has been given to Me.**   Matthew 28:18

He knew His divinity. **Philippians 2:5–7** KJV says,

> Let this mind be in you, which was also in Christ Jesus: Who, being in the form of God, thought it not robbery to be equal with God: But made himself of no reputation, and took upon him the form of a servant, and was made in the likeness of men:

Even though He was God, He laid aside divinity and became a man. He was 100% God and 100% man. While on earth He had to defeat the devil as a man, totally dependent on God. Living a sinless life then qualified Him to die for our sins.

Going to the river

When Jesus went to the Jordan River to be baptized, His divinity was confirmed by the Father. The Holy Spirit came down on Him in the form of a dove, and a voice from heaven proclaimed, "This is my beloved Son, in whom I am well pleased; hear ye him" (Matthew 17:5 KJV). His identity as the Messiah was about to be manifested in public ministry. But it couldn't happen quite yet.

After the river comes the desert, and then comes the ministry. Water baptism symbolizes the death of self-sufficiency. Of course, Jesus never walked in self-sufficiency or sin of any kind, but He told

John that He was to be baptized to fulfill prophecy. After Jesus was baptized by John, He went to the desert. There it was confirmed who He wasn't.

In the desert

At this time, in His humanity, He wasn't in charge. He refused to compromise His position of total obedience to the Father. Although tempted, He refused to abuse the power given to Him for any selfish motive. Jesus refused to doubt the integrity of the Word of God or twist those words in order to exercise any control.

No self could be tempted to rise up in Him. By using the word self here, I'm not just referring to selfish motives, but also any form of self-will, self-confidence, or self-effort. There was no room for any of these because Jesus was filled with the Holy Spirit. That didn't mean He couldn't be tempted, though. The devil tried to make a deposit of doubt about the Father's integrity, but Jesus refused to receive it.

No doubt received means no power diminished

That seed of doubt was never put in His heart, then or at any other time. Therefore, the devil had no deposit to withdraw later. Throughout Jesus' life, He stayed in close communion with the Father and was constantly empowered by the Holy Spirit. The devil never gained any control over Him. At the proper time, Jesus allowed Himself to be arrested because it was part of God's will, not because the devil ever had the upper hand. He said that no man would take His life but that He would lay it down (John 10:18).

The submission to and dependence upon the Father that He chose at Gethsemane was really already decided long before in the desert temptation. No matter how many times or in what ways He was tempted, Jesus never diverted from complete obedience to God's will because no doubt about God's motives was ever deposited in Him. No deposit; no withdrawal. Remember, right before Jesus was arrested He said,

> **Hereafter I will not talk much with you: for the prince of this world cometh, and hath nothing in me.**
>
> John 14:30 KJV

Because the devil had nothing deposited in Jesus, the devil had no power over Him. The Amplified Version of the Bible explains His meaning more fully in the same verse.

> **I will not talk with you much more, for the prince (evil genius, ruler) of the world is coming. And he has no claim on Me. [He has nothing in common with Me; there is nothing in Me that belongs to him, and he has no power over Me.]**
>
> John 14:30

No obstruction of revelation

The last few verses in the first chapter of John's gospel tell briefly about Jesus' first meeting with Nathanael. This shows another example of the importance of an undivided heart toward God.

Look at **John 1:47–49.** What did Jesus see in this man?

> **Jesus saw Nathanael coming toward Him and said concerning him, See! Here is an Israelite indeed [a true descendant of Jacob], in whom there is no guile *nor* deceit *nor* falsehood *nor* duplicity!**
>
> **Nathanael said to Jesus, How do You know me? [How is it that You know these things about me?] Jesus answered him, Before [ever] Philip called you, when you were still under the fig tree, I saw you.**
>
> **Nathanael answered, Teacher, You are the Son of God! You are the King of Israel!**

Jesus saw a pure heart. And that pure heart had no problem seeing God. Revelation comes easily to the heart that isn't wearing the dark glasses of doubt. That's what Jesus saw: no duplicity, no extra layer. A heart like that does not interfere with the continuous flow of **seeking**, **revelation**, **obedience**, and **transformation**.

Why river and desert before ministry

We cannot be 100% committed until we are 100% convinced about the motives and character of God. That's why the river should come first. That is the place where the assurance comes. That assurance then goes with us into any desert we face. And it is that assurance that makes it possible for us to go on through to the Promised Land instead of dying in the desert.

This pattern of river, desert, and ministry is a necessary progression. In the river, we receive God's power and affirmation. In the desert, we settle the self issues.

We become like John the Baptist who cried out as a voice in the wilderness. We cry out in the wilderness of our broken heart, "I'm preparing the way of the Lord in my life. I give up self-sufficiency for God-sufficiency. I won't try to protect myself or say God brought me out here to die, like the Israelites said in the desert. I will say God is my refuge and strength. He gives rivers in the desert. He makes me well able to come through this and take whatever land (ministry) He gives me because it is not me but *Christ in me, the hope of glory*" (Colossians 1:27).

The power of total dependence

We need to know who we are and who we aren't. God resists the proud and gives grace to the humble (1 Peter 5:5). Grace is enabling power. Who gets it? The humble. Who are the humble? Those who know who they aren't. They will not abuse God's anointing. They can be trusted with power.

I love the faith teachings that help us see a good God who blesses His children and gives them power and authority. Some have looked down on these teachings and called them arrogant. These critics don't understand that the secret of this power we have in the New Covenant is total dependence on God.

Remember, the lesson of the Old Covenant is that we can't do it. The secret power of the New Covenant is that everything is to be done by God Himself! There is no room for arrogance in that.

Andrew Murray said, "There is the God of love waiting to do everything in him who is willing to be nothing."[7] John the Baptist said, "He must increase, but I must decrease" (John 3:30). He also said, "Prepare the way of the Lord" (John 1:23). Let's make room for God's power to work in us and through us.

We make room for Him by laying down self-will and all confidence in our own efforts. That's pretty scary, but it's not as scary as trying to do it ourselves. Even so, we hate to give up control unless God can really be trusted to have our best interests in mind. He can! **2 Corinthians 3:17–18** KJV tells us,

> **Now the Lord is that Spirit: and where the Spirit of the Lord *is*, there *is* liberty.**
> **But we all, with open face beholding as in a glass the glory of the Lord, are changed into the same image from glory to glory, *even* as by the Spirit of the Lord.**

Our God image determines our self-image, who we see ourselves as being in Christ. Remember, we will progressively become who we see ourselves as being. When we see ourselves as safe and strong because of our submission to and dependence on Jesus, then we become truly useful. The dance takes on a new security, humility, and power.

To the world

Jesus left the desert full of the power of the Holy Spirit. He came to Nazareth and went to the synagogue and stood up to read. He had done this many times, but this time was different. He read from Isaiah 61 about the coming of the Messiah.

> **The Spirit of the Lord is upon me, because he hath anointed me to preach the gospel to the poor; he hath sent me to heal the brokenhearted, to preach deliverance to the captives, and recovering of sight to the blind, to set at liberty them that are bruised,**
> **To preach the acceptable year of the Lord.**
>
> Luke 4:18–19 KJV

Don't you think that those present sensed something unusual at the hearing of these words when read by their Author and Finisher? He had often read scripture to them before, but this reading came after He had been to the river and the desert. The Spirit *was* upon Him in a new way. He closed the book and sat down. They were all still staring at Him, wondering why He seemed so different, so powerful. He said, "This day is this scripture fulfilled in your ears." They were stunned. They had just heard the words of either the Messiah or a blasphemer.

He was ready. From that time on, there were miracles and persecution. But nothing was to stop Him—no praise, no pain. He had been to the river. He had been to the desert. He knew who He was and who He wasn't. He was God the Son landed on earth, as an earthling (the Word made flesh), carrying out a heavenly mission. That mission would continue until He said, "It is finished!"

We too can finish our mission and say like Paul:

> **I have fought a good fight, I have finished *my* course, I have kept the faith.**
>
> 2 Timothy 4:7 KJV

He'll take us to the river, to the desert, and then to the world.

Wineskins and Patches

atthew's gospel records an intriguing conversation between Jesus and the disciples of John the Baptist. They asked Him about the differences between His ministry and John's ministry. His answer was not a comprehensive teaching but a brief explanation about how the Old and New Covenants don't mix.

> And no one puts a piece of cloth that has not been shrunk on an old garment, for such a patch tears away from the garment and a worse rent (tear) is made.
> Neither is new wine put in old wineskins; for if it is, the skins burst and are torn in pieces, and the wine is spilled and the skins are ruined. But new wine is put into fresh wineskins, and so both are preserved.
>
> **Matthew 9:16–17**

Another time when Jesus spoke of John the Baptist in connection with the contrast between the Old and New Covenants is found in Luke's gospel.

> **I tell you, among those born of women there is no one greater than John; but he that is inferior [to the other citizens] in the kingdom of God is greater [in comparable privilege] than he.**
> Luke 7:28

It is interesting to note that the brief time when Jesus and John the Baptist were both on earth was a unique time of transition when the Old and New Covenants overlapped. Both John and Jesus had supernatural circumstances and angelic announcements involved with their births and names. John, the last of the Old Testament prophets, was born to a very old woman apparently too late. And Jesus was born to a very young woman apparently too early.

John's life marked the end of the Old Covenant, the way God dealt with man before Christ. God's Old Covenant with man was neither bad nor unnecessary, but the New Covenant was much better. That's why Jesus explains in the preceding scripture that the best the Old Covenant had to offer was still inferior to the least that the New Covenant offers.

John was born for one reason—to usher in Jesus. The Old Covenant existed only to usher in the New Covenant. This is not only true in history but also in our lives. Law and grace are totally incompatible. We were never meant to be remodeled, but replaced. The old and new don't mix.

Jesus said that He did not come to destroy the law but to fulfill it (Matthew 5:17). Much of the ceremonial part of the law, like the system of animal sacrifice, was finished when Jesus came and made the ultimate sacrifice. Ceremonial law, which symbolized what Jesus would do, was no longer needed; but God's moral standards will never go away. God wasn't against sin in the Old Covenant and then got over it in the New Covenant. Grace is not divine leniency.

Holiness is just as important in the New Covenant as it was in the Old. However, the way that those of us in Christ relate to God and grow in character is far different and far better. We can relate to

God differently in the New Covenant because of the regeneration of our spirits at the new birth.

New creation versus dual-nature

The question is: Are you a new creature in Christ (2 Corinthians 5:17) or a sinner impersonating a saved person? But, you may say, nobody's perfect. Aren't we all in a process? Aren't we all sinners saved by grace? No, we are all sinners *or* saved by grace!

On the surface, this may sound confusing. However, it's not irrelevant or a bunch of theological hair splitting. We have been exposed to a lot preaching that encourages us to see ourselves as having two natures or identities. The good us and the bad us are presented as continually fighting for control.

Certain scriptures seem to support this dual-nature theory. It is beyond the scope of this book to go into a detailed study of how various Greek words are translated in various passages of Paul's writings. I will only address this identity issue briefly in light of one commonly misunderstood portion of scripture.

The confusion seems to come when we don't differentiate between the *sin nature*, which we get rid of at salvation, and plain old *human nature*, which we're still stuck with as human beings on this planet. We don't cease to be human when we get saved, but the change in our identity as new creatures in Christ is much more literal than most Christians realize. Is all this really important in studying holiness? Extremely.

The flesh (human nature not anxious to change) is comfortable with the dual-nature concept. If we are not really able to change, then how could God hold us responsible for weakness beyond our control? Surely He would understand that we are doing the best we can. This is where a lot of preaching goes with the seventh chapter of Romans.

> For I know that nothing good dwells within me, that is, in my flesh. I can will what is right, but I cannot perform it. [I have the intention and urge to do what is right, but no power to carry it out.]
>
> For I fail to practice the good deeds I desire to do, but the evil deeds that I do not desire to do are what I am [ever] doing.
>
> Romans 7:18–19

Many identify with Paul's discussion about trying to do what's right and not being able to. Some who struggle with sin love to point out that the great apostle Paul shared their struggle. But did he?

Paul never intended to console anyone with a message of despair. He's not saying, "Don't worry about being in bondage to sin. I am too. We're all in the same boat until we get to heaven." No. His message is quite the opposite.

I challenge you to read the sixth and eighth chapters of Romans and conclude that Paul, as he describes himself in those chapters, was a man constantly struggling with sin. It's not there. We see only a triumphant Paul, fully able to boldly carry out his call in the power of the resurrected Christ.

Is there a contradiction here? No, because the Paul described in Romans 7 is Paul B.C. (before Christ). Here we see a man zealous for God, doing his best, but still powerless against sin. In spite of all his good intentions and great efforts, Paul was unable to walk in consistent victory over sin, until he had a born-again experience (to do away with the sin nature) and received the power of the Holy Spirit.

Paul was trying to make us understand two things:

- the insufficiency of man's own efforts to combat sin, and
- the total sufficiency that is available to us in the power of Christ.

Paul wasn't trying to let us off the hook about sin. He was trying to show us the way out. He said, "Who will deliver me?" and then he answered that question with, "Jesus will."

Over and over in the writings of Paul throughout the New Testament, we find the reoccurring theme of our identity in Christ. Paul wasn't just discussing theology. He knew that if we don't know the power that's available to us as born-again, Spirit-filled people, then we will not be able to walk in it. If we don't know who we really *are*, we will go on acting like someone we're *not*—sinners.

First, we are delivered from our sin nature. At the time of conversion, when we accepted Jesus, our identity changed. Our spirit (the real us) became new, not remodeled, added to, or temporarily whitewashed, but *new.*

Then, our mind, will, and emotions have to catch up as we walk out our new identity. A lot of old patterns leave as our spirit takes control over our soul. Our spirit, in constant contact with the Holy Spirit in us, reprograms our personality.

The enabling power of God's grace flows out of our spirit and gives orders as we grow in Christ and renew our mind in the Word. Our spirit says, "Look here, **mind,** everything's different now and here's how you're going to think. Look here, **will,** you're not calling the shots any more. You are submitted to the will of Christ and I'll be telling you what He wants. And look here, **emotions,** don't tell me how you feel all the time, because I'm going to be telling you how to feel about things from now on."

It's still a foreign concept to many Christians to think that they can have power over their own personalities, their own human nature. Our *human nature,* with all its frailties, doesn't disappear when we are born again. It's the *sin nature* that goes. That was the thing that couldn't and didn't want to follow God.

With the sin nature gone, our human nature is quite change-able. The power of the Holy Spirit *is* sufficient. That's what Paul preached. That was the power of the early church.

They knew who they were in Christ. Those of us who struggle with sin today need that revelation. We think we have a sin prob-lem; but, in reality, we have an identity problem.

Of course, we are in a transformation process, but it's important to know what we are becoming. Are we trying to become something we're not yet? No, we are becoming who we already *are* in Him. In Him is everything we need—righteousness, peace, and joy.

So what about all the distractions—the world, the flesh, the devil? Does Jesus have power over all these? Are you in Him? Then pull rank! Keep the flesh under subjection and take authority over the enemy.

> I have told you these things, so that in Me you may have [per-fect] peace *and* confidence. In the world you have tribulation *and* trials *and* distress *and* frustration; but be of good cheer [take courage; be confident, certain, undaunted]! For I have overcome the world. [I have deprived it of power to harm you and have con-quered it for you.]
>
> John 16:33

To operate in this kind of overcoming life takes continual seek-ing, continual abiding in the vine. We've got to stay connected to our source, stay seeking!

Seeking and serving

Our biggest challenge is not in our doing for Jesus, but it is in our personal seeking, our abiding in Him. An example of this is found in the familiar story of Martha and Mary. Once when Jesus was staying with these friends, Martha became anxious about get-ting practical things done.

Jesus had also talked to some other people who were concerned about practical things (food and clothing). Jesus told them to seek first the Kingdom of God and not to be anxious (Matthew 6:33–34). His answer to Martha about Mary was similar. He told Martha that she was worried about many things, but only one was needed: the better portion that Mary had chosen—seeking!

At first glance it would seem that Martha, doing everything she could to serve Jesus, was the most unselfish one. Mary, on the other hand, just flopped down at His feet wanting to hear His teachings (a little nervy, considering that women were not even supposed to study the law in those days).

Which sister was Jesus more impressed with? Mary. Why? Jesus was not just looking at their usefulness that day. Martha may have appeared more productive on that day, but what about the next day?

By then Mary is not even really the same person. The very life of God had been imparted into her by what she had learned and the deeper level she had come to know Him. She had entered into the dance (seeking, revelation, obedience, transformation). Martha, on the other hand, had gained only a little more practice in cooking and cleaning by the next day.

But, you may say, what Martha was doing was good and it was for Jesus. Yes, but notice, He did not just call for balance. He clearly took Mary's side. He didn't just want their labor; He wanted *them*!

He knew that if they skipped the **seeking** and the **revelation** and just went on to **obedience**, it would not be the kind of **obedience** that is a response to **revelation**. And, therefore, it would not be the kind of **obedience** that leads to **transformation**.

Relating to Christ is not a job description. It's more of an apprenticeship, where one always watches the master (seeking, abiding). Jesus was always watching the Father. He said, "The Son can do nothing of himself, but what he seeth the Father do" (John 5:19 KJV).

Mary was a seeker, an abider. Spirit-led, Spirit-empowered obedience (service) is the natural result of that kind of relationship.

Look at how Mary related to Jesus much later on one evening a few days just before his death. In the twelfth chapter of John we see Jesus with this family again. They made Him supper. Martha served the food. Again we see Mary at Jesus' feet, this time not to receive but to give, not in the **seeking** part of the dance but in the **obeying** part.

She poured rare, expensive perfume on His feet and dried them with her hair. It was a beautiful expression of worship that only she and He fully understood. She seemed to grasp what was going to happen to Him and how to serve Him at that time in a way that those around her couldn't.

How did she get such **revelation**? Much **seeking** had led to much **transformation**. This sacred act of devotion was not just doing something. It was a part of the natural flow of the dance. It was an expression of who she was, who she had become in Him. You see, you can *do* without *being*. But you cannot *be* without *doing*!

Seven

Revelation—Who Gets It?

[Things are hidden temporarily only as a means to revelation.] For there is nothing hidden except to be revealed, nor is anything [temporarily] kept secret except in order that it may be made known.

Mark 4:22

he Parable of the Sower is about revelation from God. In a way it is the mother of all parables because it is a parable about parables, a teaching about veiled truth. Jesus said to His disciples,

Do you not discern *and* understand this parable? How then is it possible for you to discern *and* understand all the parables?

Mark 4:13

Why do some people receive revelation from God and others don't? Are some just not supposed to get it? Certain words of Jesus could be taken that way.

And He said to them, To you has been entrusted the mystery of the kingdom of God [that is, the secret counsels of God which are hidden from the ungodly]; but for those outside [of our circle] everything becomes a parable.

Mark 4:11

On the surface as we read this verse, and similar ones in Luke 8:10 and Matthew 13:11, we could think God gives revelation to some and not others. It would appear that some are supposed to get it and some can't, and that's all there is to it. But obviously there's more to it. God doesn't just arbitrarily enlighten some and leave others in the dark. Listen to Jesus' words as He introduces His explanation of the Parable of the Sower.

> And He replied to them, To you it has been given to know the secrets *and* mysteries of the kingdom of heaven, but to them it has not been given.
> For whoever has [spiritual knowledge], to him will more be given *and* he will be furnished richly so that he will have abundance; but from him who has not, even what he has will be taken away.
> This is the reason that I speak to them in parables: because having the power of seeing, they do not see; and having the power of hearing, they do not hear, nor do they grasp *and* understand.
> In them indeed is the process of fulfillment of the prophecy of Isaiah, which says: You shall indeed hear *and* hear but never grasp *and* understand; *and* you shall indeed look *and* look but never see *and* perceive.
> For this nation's heart has grown gross (fat and dull), *and* their ears heavy *and* difficult of hearing, *and* their eyes they have tightly closed, lest they see *and* perceive with their eyes, *and* hear *and* comprehend the sense with their ears, *and* grasp *and* understand with their heart, and turn *and* I should heal them.

Matthew 13:11–15

Verse 13 implies a choice when He says they have the power to see and hear but don't. Mark 4:12 in the Amplified Version refers to "their willful rejection of the truth." In Matthew 13:15, notice how

Jesus explains that it is their heart condition that causes them to hear but not understand.

There are those who are truly deceived because they are honestly ignorant and therefore don't believe. And then there are those who have what Hebrews 3:12 in the King James Version calls "an evil heart of unbelief." This is willful rejection of truth. Here's the same verse in the Amplified Version.

> [Therefore beware] brethren, take care, lest there be in any one of you a wicked, unbelieving heart [which refuses to cleave to, trust in, and rely on Him], leading you to turn away *and* desert *or* stand aloof from the living God.
>
> Hebrews 3:12

Interestingly, before this passage, Jesus was just referring to those who hardened their hearts in the wilderness and therefore could not enter into rest. Note that they hardened their own hearts. It wasn't just done to them. This explains Matthew 13:12 and the similar passage in **Mark 4:25** which says,

> For to him who has will more be given; and from him who has nothing, even what he has will be taken away [by force],

God not only knows who's seeking, but the motives of that person's heart. Those **seeking** God with pure motivation will find their **revelation** growing, sometimes imperceptibly like the seed referred to in **Mark 4:26–27.**

> And He said, The kingdom of God is like a man who scatters seed upon the ground,
> And then continues sleeping and rising night and day while the seed sprouts and grows *and* increases—he knows not how.

Unfortunately this principle also works in reverse. Those who harden their hearts against revelation get more deceived. The darkness gets darker instead of the light getting brighter. The deception starts with self-sufficiency, which is counterfeit wholeness. This is subtle. Counterfeits sneak up on us. We need to be careful of our motives and our focus. What we focus on affects our motives and vice versa. Jesus explains further in **Mark 4:24.**

> And He said to them, Be careful what you are hearing. The measure [of thought and study] you give [to the truth you hear] will be the measure [of virtue and knowledge] that comes back to you— and more [besides] will be given to you *who hear.*

Parables, veiled truth, become clearer to those seeking with a right heart and remain veiled to those who are not able to receive. The more we receive, the more we are able to receive.

> With many such parables [Jesus} spoke the Word to them, as they were able to hear *and* to comprehend *and* understand.
> He did not tell them anything without a parable; but private-ly to His disciples (those who were peculiarly His own) He explained everything [fully].
>
> Mark 4:33–34

Those closest to Him got extra explanation not given to the crowds. At that time, He could only be involved intimately with a few. But now, through the Holy Spirit, He is accessible to everyone, not just a few in an inner circle. Maybe that's why He said that it was better for them (and us) that He go away so that the Holy Spirit could come (John 16:7).

Here's an interesting question. If Jesus came to destroy the works of the devil (which is deception) why was He so mysterious, teach-ing so much in parables? Perhaps it was necessary to leave a path for free will. If He bombarded us with irresistible revelation, He would be in effect taking us by force. Instead He came as the Son of Man, a Bridegroom coming for His bride. He came to propose to us, not kidnap us.

But when He comes again in the second coming He will come as the Son of God, the Judge of all. What an entrance that will be!

There will be no doubt or confusion about who He is at that time. Deciding time will be over then.

But His first entrance was relatively quiet, with little fanfare. Yes, a star, some angels, some confirmation—just enough to put God's permanent signature on the event but not enough to attract much attention. He came to infiltrate the devil's territory with an irreversible invasion. The Creator came to reclaim His creation.

> **But as many as received him, to them gave he power to become the sons of God, *even* to them that believe on his name.**
> **John 1:12 KJV**

He left us here in enemy territory for a reason—to get more of those He died for. He didn't come for a privileged few but "whosoever will." The Bible says He is not willing that any should perish (2 Peter 3:9). He left us here to finish the harvest.

To the devil's horror, when Jesus died, that wasn't the end of the invasion, but only the beginning! And Jesus didn't leave us defenseless and directionless. He left us with spiritual weapons and gifts for protection and warfare and for communication with Him (headquarters). Lord, finish Your work in us and through us.

Eight

Ask Him to Remain

s a way to further explore the revelation part of the dance, let's look at three different groups of people in the New Testament. All of them were given revelation from God but they reacted very differently.

The first group

The first group was a group of Samaritans who were suddenly confronted with a startling testimony from a woman among them who excitedly claimed that she had found the Messiah. She had met Him at the well. (Incidentally, it was against tradition for Him to be speaking to any woman, much less a Samaritan. But Jesus was led by the Spirit rather than traditions of men.) In the course of her conversation with Jesus, she found that she was talking to the long-awaited Messiah. She ran back and told the people in her town.

Let's look at those townspeople that she told about this encounter. Scripture doesn't suggest that she was one who had any particular influence or credibility with the people in her town; nevertheless, they believed her.

Not only did they believe her, but they ran out and asked Him to stay with them. And He did! He stayed for two days. Why? He had found some seekers. Remember the first part of Mark 4:25: "For to him who has will more be given." Notice how they responded.

> **Now numerous Samaritans from that town believed in *and* trusted in Him because of what the woman said when she declared and testified, He told me everything that I ever did.**
>
> **So when the Samaritans arrived, they asked Him to remain with them, *and* He did stay there two days.**
>
> John 4:39–40

They responded to the original **revelation** with **obedience. Obedience** in their case meant making the effort to find out about Jesus. They were rewarded by having their original faith **transformed.** It wasn't that they didn't really believe when they first heard the woman's testimony. They did. But now they believed on a whole different level. This change is described in verse 42.

> **And they told the woman, Now we no longer believe (trust, have faith) just because of what you said; for we have heard Him ourselves [personally], and we know that He truly is the Savior of the world, *the Christ*.**
>
> John 4:42

After those two days, I imagine nobody could have convinced them that this man was not the Messiah. If He had not spent that time with them, and then later they heard someone say, "He's not the Christ," they might have thought, *Well, I guess that woman is a little unstable. Perhaps she was mistaken.* Someone once said, "The man with an argument is no match for the man with an experience." These people had experienced Jesus for themselves and they knew that they knew who He was. By their experience they owned their belief, made it solidly their own.

Some people today are suspicious of all personal revelation and experiential worship. Anything that looks emotional or unusual, they write off as some sort of fleshly thrill seeking or a play for attention. "After all," they say, "We have the Word." They think that's the only way God speaks to us today, so we should just believe the Bible and keep things decent and in order.

Certainly God speaks primarily through His Word. When He communicates by the Holy Spirit some other way, those experiences in the Spirit should not be in conflict with the written Word, but rather validate and reinforce it. In this same story Jesus tells the woman at the well that we must worship in spirit *and* in truth.

The second group

Let's move on to the second group of people. They also witnessed a dramatic testimony, but they reacted very differently. When Jesus delivered the man with the legion of demons as described in Mark 5, the word of what happened got out quickly.

Jesus had negotiated a departure of the demons out of the man into a herd of hogs. The huge herd of hogs, suddenly demon possessed, ran over a cliff into the sea and drowned. Perhaps Jesus got the hogs involved in order to trick the demons into leaving the man willingly so that the man would not be harmed by their departure.

At any rate, the men, who were there as hog feeders and saw all this, ran off and spread the word about the sudden, simultaneous suicide of their two thousand hogs and the madman's deliverance. Soon people from the town as well as the country came to see what was happening. When they saw the man they had known as a raving lunatic all dressed up normally and looking sane and happy, they were struck with fear.

Why weren't they rejoicing about this miracle? Why didn't they want to know all about Jesus like the Samaritans did when they heard about Him from the woman at the well?

I once heard someone suggest that these people were all hog farmers who didn't want Jesus killing any more of their pigs. That's an amusing interpretation but I don't agree. I believe it had to do with the condition of their hearts. Look at their reaction.

> **And they began to beg [Jesus] to leave their neighborhood.**
> **Mark 5:17**

So what did Jesus do? He left. He moved away from their hardened, unbelieving hearts and moved directly toward faith in the hearts of Jairus and the woman with the issue of blood. The power of God always moves in the direction of faith.

Faith doesn't make God act; it opens the door for the grace of God that is already provided to be manifested. Jesus, personifying the power of God, was available to the people where the madman lived. But that power was not manifested. They extended no faith even when they saw the power undeniably demonstrated. The **revelation** found no **obedience,** and so there was no **transformation** in those people. They missed the hour of their visitation.

The third group

The third group of people that I want to call to your attention is a group of Jews who came to hear Paul explain his testimony and his belief in Jesus. Their reaction when confronted with the power of God was not unanimous like the other two groups. In this third group, they all heard the same words but look what happened.

> **So when they had set a day with him, they came in large numbers to his lodging. And he fully set forth and explained the matter to them from morning until night, testifying to the king-**

dom of God and trying to persuade them concerning Jesus both from the Law of Moses *and* from the Prophets.

And some were convinced and believed what he said, *and* others did not believe.

Acts 28:23–24

This group disagreed among themselves. Some believed and some didn't. As they left, Paul quoted to them Isaiah 6:9–10, which is about people who cannot believe because they have hardened their hearts.

And so we've seen three groups of people. One group asked Jesus to remain. Another bunch asked Him to leave. And in this last story, we see the Word taking root in the soil of some men's hearts, but not in others. Those who didn't believe must have been like the soil along the path where the seed fell but birds came and ate it up. Jesus explains this portion of the Parable of the Sower in Mark 4:15. This was the soil where the seed never took root even temporarily.

The ones along the path are those who have the Word sown [in their hearts], but when they hear, Satan comes at once and [by force] takes away the message which is sown in them.

Mark 4:15

If the heart is too hard to hold the seed, it can easily be taken away. Heart conditions make all the difference. Why else would Nathaniel, after hearing only a few words from Jesus say, "You are the Son of God, the King of Israel," and the Pharisees, after seeing Him perform many miracles still say, "You are a blasphemer"?

When the power of God is present, some run to the altar and some run to the nearest exit. Have you ever been in a meeting of believers when the power of God was manifested and you could sense the tension between the reactions of the people? For some, what was happening was too much; and for others, it was not enough. Those hungering and thirsting after righteousness wanted to be filled, wanted Him to remain. At the same time, those who only wanted religion were not comfortable with Him showing up in any unpredictable or uncontrollable way.

God's turning up the heat! He's showing up wherever He's welcomed. He comes to comfort the afflicted and afflict the comfortable. We are not only going to see the lost saved, but many of the religious will trade in their fig leaves (a symbol of religion) for a permanent place in the vine.

Dancing on the Water

Asking Jesus to remain in New Covenant context means abiding in the vine as Jesus teaches us in John 15. Just because we are a saved person with the Holy Spirit in our spirit doesn't mean that the power of God is always working in our lives.

We are either walking in the Spirit or the flesh—the supernatural or the natural. Salvation was all God. So is sanctification. When we let it be all Him and we're just connected to His power, abiding in the vine, fruit happens.

When Peter walked on the water, he knew he was undertaking something totally supernatural. He knew he couldn't do such a thing on his own. He couldn't even help except to step out. In stepping out, he added **obedience** to his **revelation**. For a while he had **transformation**. He was participating in a miracle!

Then something went wrong. He was suddenly manpowered instead of God-powered. He lost his connection, got disoriented, and started sinking. What happened?

He looked at the wind and the waves. He was suddenly afraid that he couldn't do it. The truth is that he never was doing it. He couldn't have pulled off anything like that no matter how calm the day or flat the sea.

When you think about it, the storm was hilariously irrelevant! There could not have been a day with weather favorable enough for

Peter to do it by himself. Also, there could not be a storm big enough or bad enough to keep Jesus from empowering Peter to do it.

The only way it couldn't work was if Peter stopped abiding. He took his eyes off of his source, or perhaps the waves got high enough to block his view of Jesus. He slipped into self-sufficiency, and God can't empower self-sufficiency. Self-sufficiency always leads to sinking. He lost his **transformation** because he lost his original **revelation** that this was all Jesus' doing. He got scared and began to think, *what if I can't do this?*

The answer came in the sinking. He instantly got another revelation: "You *can't* do this, dummy. Get ahold of your source—*He* was doing it all." He cried out to Jesus and immediately he was back in the dance. They walked on the water again back to the boat.

He remains as we believe

Peter discovered that the secret to finishing strong is staying focused on Jesus, remembering that it's all Him. What if He really did it all? What would be left for us to do? Only believe.

> They then said, What are we to do, that we may [habitually] be working the works of God? [What are we to do to carry out what God requires?]
> Jesus replied, This is the work (service) that God asks of you: that you believe in the One Whom He has sent [that you cleave to, trust, rely on, and have faith in His Messenger].
>
> John 6:28–29

Step out on grace

No more pressure! No more worrying if our performance measures up. Lord, if it really is all you, bid us to come to you on the water of grace. It feels like we're stepping out on nothing because we're so used to holding ourselves up. But we've been standing on a lie. Our works can't hold us up no matter how hard we try. And no storm is too much for You to walk us through.

You're the solid rock we stand on, and all other ground really is sinking sand. We can finally rest. Believing is easy, Jesus, when we're believing in Your ability to hang on to us instead of our ability to hang on to You!

Nine

You Might Be
a Legalist If—

aw and grace are opposite and cannot coexist. It is like the new wine in old wineskins or the new patch on old cloth. Paul taught a lot about us being under grace instead of law. This is hard for many to understand since we know that God's moral standards are not relaxed in the New Covenant. If anything, according to the words of Jesus, New Covenant standards are higher because they deal with motives as well as outward behavior. In the Sermon on the Mount (Matthew 5) Jesus speaks plainly about motives.

So what is legalism? Here's a description by Steve McVey from his book *Grace Rules* that may surprise you.

> *It was my belief that if a Christian committed himself to obeying the Word of God, he would be blessed by God. That, however, is the perfect description of a legalistic Christian lifestyle. It is an*

attempt to gain God's blessings and to make spiritual progress by what we do. It is a description of a life ruled by law, not grace.[8]

You see, it's not a matter of just staying out of sin. Sin is a symptom of a problem, not the source or the root of the problem. Abiding in Christ is not just following a list of rules; it is trusting Him to live in and through us.

> **For the kingdom of God is not meat and drink; but righteousness, and peace, and joy in the Holy Ghost.**
> **Romans 14:17** KJV

Legalism is subtle. Self-sufficiency, walking in the flesh instead of abiding in Christ, is expressed in one of two ways: rebellion or religion.

The rebel is a backslider. This is not subtle. This is someone who knows that he's doing wrong but chooses to do it anyway. But the religious departure from abiding is more unintentional and so more insidious.

The rebel knows he's a rebel even if he doesn't want to repent. But the legalist does not know he is a legalist. His life may look very good. How can we ever know if we are into law instead of grace? Try taking the righteousness, peace, and joy test.

YOU MIGHT BE A LEGALIST IF—

- No matter how hard you try or how well you are doing, you still feel that you've not done enough. You're consistently disappointed with your performance as a Christian and feel that God is too, even though He loves you.

- You don't have consistent peace. There is an undefined anxiety even when you are not aware of a specific threat.

- You don't have consistent joy. There is an undefined sadness underlying even the happy times.

If you identify with any of the above, you may indeed be a legalist—one who is relying on manpower instead of God-power. Remember that grace is not only unmerited favor but also God's enabling power.

In current psychological terminology, a person is sometimes called an "enabler." By this we mean someone who enables someone else to continue in a destructive behavior pattern by always intervening to cover their tracks. By constantly fixing the circumstances and cleaning up the messes, the enabler may not be helping the deceived person at all in the long run.

The deceived person is living some sort of lie (for example, thinking he is not really an alcoholic). If someone else causes the circumstances to seem to support the lie that there is no problem, then the deceived person is "enabled" to continue on under the deception and control of the lie.

The lie of legalism says: We can, by our own strength, live holy lives if we try hard enough. That is self-sufficiency. And God can't enable it. If He did, He would be propping up a lie, and that lie is pride. Instead God gives grace (enabling power) to the humble—those who have a revelation of their own weakness.

What went wrong?

How do we slip into legalism? Most new Christians seem to enjoy a sweet simplicity in Christ. Then we get into traditions, which may not be bad in themselves. Those traditions (how we do our religious activities) become the wrappings for our relationship with Jesus.

If we are not careful, we shift our focus from the content of the packaging (Jesus) to the packaging itself (what we are doing for Him). We can get so busy worshiping the wrappings that at first we don't notice that they're empty. Ichabod means the glory of God has departed. It is somewhat like they used to say at the end of an Elvis concert, "Ladies and gentlemen, the King has left the building."

We find ourselves left with lifeless religion. What happened? We were doing it without Him and He could no longer anoint or enable our efforts.

More works won't work

So what do we do next? Quick, find some fig leaves. We try more professionalism, more hype, better programs, bigger buildings—but it's still powerless. Turning up the manpower doesn't work. Polishing our performance won't bring back the anointing.

Stepping up our evangelistic outreach is not the solution either. Granted, winning people to Christ is exciting and new Christians, with their contagious zeal, are encouraging to have around. However, it's backwards thinking to expect new converts to bring life back into a dry church.

That makes about as much sense as having babies to save a marriage. It not only doesn't work but it's unfair to the babies. Throw a new, on-fire, baby Christian into a group of lukewarm Christians and the new convert will likely cool off before he can have much influence on the whole group. We are supposed to be ready to inspire new believers by our lives.

God will have to fix the older brothers' attitude before He can bring home all the prodigals. The Father wants us to be ready to run down the road with Him to greet the lost and backslidden when they come home. We should be white hot and ready to show them by our love and lives how to transition from the pigpen to the

Father's house, not how to trade in their sinful flesh for religious flesh.

Don't sink—drink

We are the Laodicean church and Jesus is outside knocking. The scene is described in the last part of Revelation chapter 3. What is Jesus doing outside of our churches and our lives? Why is He out there knocking? Didn't He say that He would never leave us or forsake us? Actually, we left Him when we turned back to self-sufficiency. He can't enable that. We got spit out of His mouth, or are at least on the verge of being spit (considering Revelation 3:16).

Many in the lukewarm church don't know He's out there knocking because they don't know He left. People in some stages of legalism can't hear Him knocking. In comparison to these, if you know you are spiritually dry and empty, then you are actually blessed because at least you know. Knowing your need, you will be excited to open the door like the woman looking for her beloved in the Song of Solomon.

We must call on the Holy Spirit like Peter when he was sinking called on Jesus. The Holy Spirit will always point us back to the person of Jesus. Then when Jesus comes back, with His presence always comes His power and everything we need—righteousness, peace, and joy. We buy it all with His grace. His grace is our alpha and omega—the only way we start and finish the dance.

> And He [further] said to me, It is done! I am the Alpha and the Omega, the Beginning and the End. To the thirsty I [Myself] will give water without price from the fountain (springs) of the water of Life.
>
> **Revelation 21:6**

Ten

Morning Star Rising

This I say then, Walk in the Spirit, and ye shall not fulfill the lust of the flesh.

For the flesh lusteth against the Spirit, and the Spirit against the flesh: and these are contrary the one to the other: so that ye cannot do the things that ye would.

But if ye be led of the Spirit, ye are not under the law.

Galatians 5:16–18 KJV

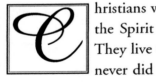hristians who consistently walk in the flesh instead of the Spirit have unhappy, unfulfilled, powerless lives. They live unchanged and unempowered and say God never did much for them. This is dysfunctional, disoriented Christianity. It may be enough to keep them out of hell, because they trusted in the blood of Jesus to save them. But they then set out to finish in the flesh what they started in the Spirit, just like the foolish Galatians.

Are ye so foolish? having begun in the Spirit, are ye now made perfect by the flesh?

Galatians 3:3 KJV

So how can we get strong in the Lord and stay consistent? How can we stay in the dance and grow in grace? Let's look at the nature of spiritual disorientation.

You cannot walk in the Spirit and walk in the flesh at the same time. They are two incompatible spiritual conditions, or positions. We are either growing in grace or losing our grip on it. Trying to be in two different spiritual positions at the same time is like trying to be in two different physical positions at once. Just try standing up and sitting down at the same time. The closest we can come is to switch back and forth from one position to the other as fast as we can, but we can't be in both positions simultaneously.

What would happen if we stood and sat alternately as quickly as possible for a long period of time? We would become disoriented. We would lose our focus. Everything would seem crazy because we would have lost our frame of reference, our familiar visual land-marks, and our sense of balance.

The same thing happens when we get spiritually disoriented. After switching back and forth from Spirit to flesh for a long time, we no longer know where we are. We don't know if we're in the Spirit or the flesh, religion or relationship, conviction or condemnation, dying to self or just dying.

The snowball effect

If we walk consistently in the flesh, or go back and forth from Spirit to flesh all the time, we will get more and more spiritually disoriented. The more confused we get, the less able we are to see truth clearly and hear the Lord's leading.

But the good news is that the more we stay in the Spirit, the more "oriented" we become. Think about the various "orientation" meetings you've attended. Some teacher or leader stood up and introduced themselves and set forth the common goals and vision of the group.

The natural progression shown in the spirit dance teaching (**seeking, revelation, obedience**, and **transformation**) is like one long orientation adventure with God. The more oriented we get, the more natural it is to **obey**.

In the process, we can't help but take on more of His nature, thoughts, and character traits. These are the fruit of the Spirit. As the **transformation** and orientation progress, the **seeking** gets easier. Everything is then flowing the right way. The light is getting brighter!

Dancing in the light

Look at what Peter says about spiritual orientation. Here's a beautiful scripture about the light getting brighter. The whole first chapter of 2 Peter is rich teaching about growing in Christ. Toward the end of the chapter, Peter is talking about being an eyewitness on the Mount of Transfiguration. This profound experience of being "together with Him on the holy mountain" made his **revelation** of Jesus even stronger. He goes on to explain poetically in verse 19 that if we **seek** the Lord in the Word, then Jesus will become more and more real to us.

> And we have the prophetic word [made] firmer still. You will do well to pay close attention to it as to a lamp shining in a dismal (squalid and dark) place, until the day breaks through [the gloom] and the Morning Star rises (comes into being) in your hearts.
>
> 2 Peter 1:19

The Word of God is our anchor. Our personal experiences with the Lord can make the Word "firmer still" to us, but they cannot contradict the Word. The Word is the plumb line we use to measure everything. **Psalms 119:105** says,

Your Word is a lamp to my feet and a light to my path.

When we walk in the light that we have, we will then get more light (**revelation**).

Dancing in the dark

With tragedies in life comes spiritual disorientation. We can be going along just fine with the light getting brighter, and suddenly experience spiritual blackout. (Sometimes this can happen even without any apparent cause.) The Word of God can sustain us through any horrible, unexplainable time.

It is like a pilot flying by instrument. He would rather be able to look out the window and orient himself with the view, but sometimes the view is obstructed. The pilot may see nothing but black out of his windshield. He may not be able to tell if he's right side up or upside down. He may be totally disoriented. But if he can trust his instruments, he can be safe in the storm.

The Word of God is like those instruments to us. We may go through a time when nothing seems to make sense, but we have the Word as our anchor, our landmark, our frame of reference. Nothing can separate us from the love of Christ because the Word says so (Romans 8:37–39). Even if it seems you cannot feel Him, see Him, or hear Him, know that He's still your Lord—100% good and 100% on your side.

Weeping may endure for a night, but joy comes in the morning.

Psalms 30:5

Meditate on **Psalms 43:5.** Nearly the same words are also in Psalms 42:5 and Psalms 42:11. Could it be that it's repeated for emphasis?

> **Why are you cast down, O my inner self?** *And* **why should you moan over me and be disquieted within me? Hope in God and wait expectantly for Him, for I shall yet praise Him, Who is the help of my [sad] countenance,** *and* **my God.**

Have a talk with your mind, will, and emotions (which is that inner self or soul). Tell yourself that you may not be able to praise God right now, but you will soon because you are dancing on even in the dark.

My purpose is not to get into a teaching on suffering. Basically, suffering stinks! We will have to deal with some of it but let's not idolize it. Some Christians are so passive about the pains and trials of life that they feel their job is to endure whatever comes, keep a good attitude, and suffer nobly.

These people are annoyed by preachers who say that God is a good God who wants to bless His children. The idea that the good stuff comes from God and the bad stuff comes from the devil seems too simplistic for them. They fear that if you preach God as too good, you will produce bratty believers who think they can order God around and then will be blown out of the water when things don't always turn out how they want.

This is not true. I am a believer in a totally good God. I believe I can trust Him enough to worship Him with my whole life. I've been through some spiritual blackouts and danced on. If I wasn't convinced of God's absolute goodness, I would either try to appease Him with religious activities and good works or else ignore Him. Either of these (religion or rebellion) is walking in the flesh.

As far as being blown out of the water, I agree with Mike Francen who says, "Never rewrite your theology to accommodate a

tragedy."[9] My job is not to understand everything but to stay in
Christ. Paul didn't come to the end of his life and say, "I've figured
it all out." No, he said in **2 Timothy 4:7** KJV,

> **I have fought a good fight, I have finished my course, I have
> kept the faith.**

And Paul didn't finish his course by just muddling though somehow, but with *joy*.

> **But none of these things move me, neither count I my life
> dear unto myself, so that I might finish my course with joy, and
> the ministry, which I have received of the Lord Jesus, to testify the
> gospel of the grace of God.**
>
> **Acts 20:24** KJV

We can't do what God wants us to do if we're always on the
wounded list. Survival is not enough. We need to get offensive
instead of defensive. We have important things to do for God and if
the devil is dumb enough to get in the way he's going to get clob-
bered.

A fixed fight

How much courage does it take to fight a fixed fight? A fixed
fight is one with a predetermined outcome—one in which your
opponent knows when you come out swinging, he must fall.

One time when our three children were small, Russell and I sat
around the table with them to learn a new board game. We laid
everything out on the table and Russell read all the rules out loud.
We were about to start playing when Chad announced that he had
another rule he had to tell us about.

Someone said, "You've never played this before. How do you
know another rule?"

He insisted, so we said, "Okay, then tell us."

The proclamation came with unexpected authority, "No matter what happens here, I'm going to win!"

He wanted to prearrange the outcome. His boldness was funny at the time, but I thought about his words seriously later. That same undefeatable confidence should be ours when we face the adversary who has already been defeated by our Lord.

When Jesus came out of that tomb, from that time on, there was a new rule. Every one of us who belong to Him, get to win. He took captivity captive. From that time on, the fight was forever fixed. All of hell knows it and there's nothing they can do about it!

Jesus came to destroy the works of the devil (1 John 3:8). We are to do the same works that Jesus did. So that means that we are to destroy the works of the devil, not be destroyed by the works of the devil. We don't want to be distracted by devil chasing either. However, when revival comes to individual lives and churches, people will get set free from all kinds of demonic oppressions.

It's like turning on a light in a dark room. Flipping that switch doesn't start some long showdown between light and darkness. Turning on the light automatically takes care of turning off the dark.

Eleven

Which First—Revival or Holiness?

W e all know that the church has become too much like the world. Preachers everywhere are calling for holiness among God's people. Some say the lack of holiness is holding back revival. Here's a fascinating and important question. Is the lack of holiness holding back revival or is the lack of revival holding back holiness? I believe that **we will not be equipped for revival until revival equips us!**

So how can we ever get started? How can we get oriented? Isaiah's encounter with the Lord can give us some insight. No doubt you've heard sermons from the sixth chapter of Isaiah.

This is about Isaiah seeing the Lord "high and lifted up, and His train filled the Temple." What a revelation! Isaiah goes on to describe the glorious scene where seraphim cry out declaring the Lord's holiness.

Let's observe this scene in context of the dance. What comes after **revelation**? **Obedience.** Anytime someone gets a **revelation** of the Lord's holiness, only one response is appropriate: conviction that brings repentance. Seeing God's holiness reveals to us our own unholiness by contrast. Sinful flesh (humanity) crumbles in the manifested presence of God.

Even John, the apostle who had earlier known Jesus so personally, later was overwhelmed by an encounter with Jesus. Upon facing the glorified Jesus on the Island of Patmos, John's human reaction to such unveiled power and holiness was similar to Isaiah's. In Revelation 1:17, John says, "When I saw Him I fell at His feet as if dead."

Isaiah's **obedience** in response to the **revelation** of God's holiness was repentance. He said,

> Woe is me! For I am undone and ruined, because I am a man of unclean lips, and I dwell in the midst of a people of unclean lips; for my eyes have seen the King, the Lord of hosts!
>
> Isaiah 6:5

Remember what comes after **obedience**? **Transformation**. The **transformation** happens here when an angel brings a coal from the altar and touches Isaiah's lips to bring forgiveness and cleansing. Then the dance continues as we see further **revelation** ("Whom shall I send?") and further **obedience** ("Here I am, send me."). Then the **transformation** seems to become a time of preparation (an orientation meeting) for Isaiah as he is told about the future of the people he would be sent to. They would be too hard-hearted to receive.

Conviction is a **revelation** of something that needs to change in us. That **revelation** should lead to the **obedience** of repentance which brings **transformation**. The people that Isaiah would prophesy to would never be **transformed** by God because they would not repent. They would not repent because the **revelation** that Isaiah would be giving them would not be understood. They would not understand the **revelation** because they had not been **seeking**. Their hearts were not receptive.

Do you remember the definition of the heart from Chapter Three? The heart is where who you are in your spirit and who you are in your soul come together. The heart condition is what makes salvation possible for the unbeliever, as well as sanctification possible for the believer.

The heart condition of the believer is what determines if the grace (enabling power of God) can flow out of our spirit into our soul (mind, will, and emotions). The heart is the connection between the fixed part of us (our born-again spirit) and the soul that's in need of transformation.

The hard-hearted unbeliever can't receive salvation yet because the door is shut between his spirit and his soul. The power of the Holy Spirit can't get past the unbeliever's soul into his spirit and bring regeneration.

Who is the real us?

Our spirit is the new creature in Christ where all things have already "become new" (2 Corinthians 5:17). The Holy Spirit has come into our spirit and brought God's life and righteousness. Because of this change, the real us, from then on, is as holy and acceptable to God as we will ever be. We are not working toward that position with God. We are already there.

If we start from that position of victory, knowing who we really are in Christ, then the ability and desire needed to transform our soul flows out from our spirit into our soul. Our mind can then think the way God wants it to, as we renew our mind in the Word of God. Our emotions can be healed and be made strong and healthy. Our will can happily trust God.

The way up is down

Our soul (mind, will, and emotions) is where we are "working out our salvation" as the scripture says (Philippians 2:12). The salvation already complete in our spirit should be continually changing the rest of us. So why is this not happening with so many Christians? Why do we agree in theory that holiness is important, but we can't walk it out?

I believe that one reason is that many are still stuck in Old Covenant mentality. The law, Paul said, was "our schoolmaster to bring us unto Christ, that we might be justified by faith" (Galatians 3:24 KJV). The Amplified Version gives a very descriptive translation of this concept. Here are verses 24 through 26.

> So that the Law served [to us Jews] as our trainer [our guardian, our guide to Christ, to lead us] until Christ [came], that we might be justified (declared righteous, put in right standing with God) by *and* through faith.
>
> But now that the faith has come, we are no longer under a trainer (the guardian of our childhood).
>
> For in Christ Jesus you are all sons of God through faith.
>
> Galatians 3:24–26

The law was the necessary bad news we had to get before we could receive the good news about grace. This is how Andrew Murray explains the transition.

> *The law cannot work out its purpose, except as it brings a man to lie guilty and helpless before the holiness of God. There the New Covenant finds him, and reveals that same God, in His grace accepting him and making him partaker of His holiness.* [10]

The Old and New Covenants are not just phases of history. They also represent phases in our walk with God. The lesson of the

Old Covenant is that even though we knew God's standards, we had no power to live it.

That realization set the stage for Jesus to come and make it possible for us to become new creatures in Christ. Holiness is what He does supernaturally in and through us.

Becoming the real us in Him

Even after we're saved, we must make the transition from law to grace. Knowing who we are is vital, because we will progressively become who we see ourselves as being. Who's in charge—the *fixed* you (the spirit) or the *getting-fixed* you (the soul)? If it's the *fixed* you, you will be operating with the power of God. But if you give identity and control to the *getting-fixed* part of you, then you will only feel pressure.

The bad news is that we can't do it—salvation *or* sanctification. The good news is that He wants to do it all! We enter into the dance and become like the one we're dancing with.

Let's make a deal

Conviction is a regular part of the dance. It is the **revelation** of something that the Holy Spirit wants to change in us. He is wanting us to acknowledge some particular sin or weakness and submit to supernatural change in that area. It is God working through our spirit to pull rank on our flesh. Our flesh may not be thrilled, but it knows that the end result will be good. This process is God working through our spirit.

At the same time, the devil often tries to work through our flesh. When God is telling our spirit to pull rank on our flesh, the devil may be inspiring our flesh to rise up and make a deal with our spirit. It's called condemnation. This is conviction's evil twin, a counterfeit to real conviction. Condemnation says, "How about if I bring the sacrifice of feeling bad? I'll punish myself with horrible guilt until the price is paid." The end result of this is not supernatural change, and so we end up back where we started.

The enemy does this to intercept real conviction. He doesn't want the power of God working in our lives so he arranges a counterfeit. It's called religion. It may look like a God-man encounter, but the proof is in the fruit. "He whom the Son sets free is free indeed" (John 8:36). Regular backsliding in the same area may be common but it's not normal.

But, you may be thinking, isn't feeling bad part of the process of repentance? Yes, but real, godly sorrow also comes with hope and specific help and love. It's not just a dose of vague misery with no way out.

Sometimes condemnation is just an attack to make us feel defeated about something that really is not even our fault or doing. Then there are times, like I've described above, when condemnation comes to derail real conviction by negotiating a false repentance.

It starts with God trying to shine a light on something for us. Then the flesh, not wanting to submit to change, may try to resist by going into some big denial tantrum: "I would change if I could, but I can't; so, I'll just feel awful and punish myself for a time. I'll suffer in proportion to my sin and then I can go on and try again."

That's resistance to the yoke. It's not the yoke, but the resistance to it, that is hard. If God is the power source, then to say we can't do something He asks us to do is the same as saying He can't do it. It's all Him, remember? We cannot hide behind our weaknesses. Our weakness is only a container for His strength.

Conviction helps us run toward holiness. Condemnation helps us run from it. Religion preaches condemnation and calls it holiness. No wonder it doesn't work.

Twelve

Thinking Inside the Box

he Lord first started teaching me about holiness many years ago at a time when I was not interested in it and didn't even know what it was. Russell and I were like many other young couples in the late 1970s. After receiving the baptism of the Holy Spirit, we left a church where there was no interest in such things, and began to run in charismatic circles (no double meaning intended).

We had all the books and tapes, and we toted our babies all over the country to get in any meeting where we could learn more about Jesus. It was a wonderful time of excitement and fast spiritual growth.

During this time, God began to teach me about a subject that we weren't hearing too many sermons on then. He used a word from the Holy Spirit, a lot of scripture, and as usual, my children, to teach me about sanctification.

At first, He showed me with an analogy about a box. Years later, after much more learning and living, my study of sanctification developed into the more complete teaching I call spirit dance. But, for this one chapter, go back with me to think inside the box. (You will see what I mean.)

Called to a treasure hunt

It was like a treasure hunt. God gave me some questions and then helped me find the answers. However, He didn't just hand them to me nonchalantly. He wanted me to pursue Him in this.

It wasn't like He was hiding something from me. He just kept backing away, beckoning me to come further, kind of like the way we coax our wobbling infant into taking her first steps by keeping our outstretched arms just a little beyond her reach. But first He had to get my attention.

I noticed a reoccurring phrase in my new prayer language (tongues). I was curious about what it meant and when I asked the Lord, to my surprise, I suddenly knew. The interpretation was only three words, "Consecrate me, Christ."

How odd. I wondered what in the world consecration was. I thought it meant something like dedication. *But isn't that something that we have to do?* I thought, *Don't we have to dedicate, or consecrate, ourselves to God? If so, then why does the Holy Spirit have me praying for Jesus to consecrate me?* I was confused but fascinated.

I plunged into scripture because I knew that any personal revelation had to be confirmed by the Word of God. When I found **1 Thessalonians 5:23–24**, I became very excited. Wow! Look who's consecrating who in this one.

> **And may the God of peace Himself sanctify you through and through [separate you from profane things, make you pure and wholly consecrated to God]; and may your spirit and soul and body be preserved sound and complete [and found] blameless at the coming of our Lord Jesus Christ (the Messiah).**

Faithful is He Who is calling you [to Himself] and utterly trustworthy, and He will also do it [fulfill His call by hallowing and keeping you].

I was rather amused to find myself studying holiness. I had no interest in the subject before. In fact, I thought it was an outdated doctrine because my only association with the word *holiness* was a bunch of legalistic dress codes and hairstyles. We joked about those poor ladies who weren't allowed to wear make-up or slacks and were always in *bundage* as far as their hair was concerned. And we laughed about how holiness couldn't have anything to do with going without make-up because the Bible says things like, "be ye kind one to another" and "avoid the appearance of evil."

I began to realize that I only knew what holiness wasn't, but I had no idea what it was. Webster's dictionary wasn't very helpful. It defined *consecrate* as "to declare something to be holy; to dedicate to sacred uses."

As I searched my Bible, I found a group of words that all seemed to overlap in their meanings and sort of define each other. These synonyms were consecration, sanctification, dedication, holiness, and being set apart.

This trying to understand *holiness* was beginning to irritate me. I was going in circles, like when you look up a word in the dictionary and it's defined by another word that you don't know. So you look up that second word only to find it defined by the original word!

Treasure found

I got busy with other things and tabled the search. Then one day, the revelation came when I wasn't even looking for it. Sometimes things come that way, like a butterfly you can't catch when you're chasing, but then it lands on your shoulder when you least expect it.

I was wrapping Christmas presents when my four-year-old flew into the room and hurled a weird question at me. "Mom, guess what I'm going to give the devil for Christmas?"

"What!?"

"I'm going to give him this...and this...and this!" he snarled toughly while slashing the air with a wild series of karate chops and kicks, little arms and legs whizzing in all directions.

I smiled, thinking that he was picking up a lot from some recent sermons we'd heard on spiritual warfare. Wanting to make sure he stayed as much pro-Jesus as he was anti-devil, I decided to challenge him with a question.

I said, "That's great, Chad. But think about this for a second. What if you could give Jesus something for Christmas? What would you give Him?"

He stopped flailing around and stared intently in full concentration. I wondered what options he was considering. After a few seconds his face brightened and he said, "I know what I'd do. I'd wrap up a big box and crawl inside it and give Him—ME."

"That's it!" I said, "That's what I've been trying to understand. That's consecration! It's so simple after all." Doesn't the Bible say that we are not our own because we were bought with a price (1Corinthians 6:19–20)? If you give someone a gift, then the new owner takes full control of that gift.

We give our lives to Jesus like putting ourselves in a box. What all would be in that box? It would contain our past, present, future, hopes, dreams, disappointments, attitudes, habits, abilities, everything we are—good, bad, and ugly.

It would be a box of broken pieces, mostly. We just say, "Here's the whole mess, Lord. Can you fix it?" We know He can, but what do we have to do?

Holy Spirit reconstruction

A lot of things started making sense. First of all, we can't leave anything out of the box. If we did, we'd be giving Him an incomplete kit to reconstruct us with. We can't just give Him Sunday morning and a few other things and expect Him to make something wonderful out of our lives.

After we give Him the box, He begins to recreate the contents. He will put some new pieces in and take some out. Other things in our box He may polish up for His glory or adjust because they've gotten twisted.

He's got a lot of changing to do, but none of those changes can be made without a decision to cooperate on our part. He can't override our free will. But, also, we can't really change ourselves. He must supply the power.

Revelation exploded in me. I began to see Jesus not just as the savior, but also the sanctifier. He's not just the Author, but the Finisher of our faith. We are so totally dependent on God to do anything, including changing ourselves. If we become the person He created us to be, it will be because we looked to Him. As we **seek**, He **reveals**. As we **obey**, He **transforms**.

> **Looking unto Jesus the author and finisher of *our* faith.**
> **Hebrews 12:2** KJV

So consecration is the giving of our whole lives to God for Him to change and use. It's too bad we can't just go throw ourselves on an altar somewhere and get up sanctified. We can't because it's a process, a wonderful adventure. Many have debated whether sanctification is an event or a process. It is both.

It all starts with giving Him the box. We can't swim across a pool until we jump in. Once in, we're all in and all His and the process begins. That's what this being *a living sacrifice* is all about.

I appeal to you therefore, brethren, *and* beg of you in view of [all] the mercies of God, to make a decisive dedication of your bodies [presenting all your members and faculties] as a living sacrifice, holy (devoted, consecrated) and well pleasing to God, which is your reasonable (rational, intelligent) service *and* spiritual worship.

Romans 12:1

Consecrate me, Christ.

Thirteen

The Yoke's on Us

Come unto me, all *ye* that labor and are heavy laden, and I will give you rest.

Take my yoke upon you, and learn of me; for I am meek and lowly in heart: and ye shall find rest unto your souls.

For my yoke *is* easy, and my burden is light.

Matthew 11:28–30 KJV

These words of Jesus are an invitation to the dance. In these verses we are told that we can rest even as we learn of Him and it doesn't have to be hard. Many believers lose their rest because they don't mix faith with their consecration. They believe in the importance of a holy life but don't believe that such a life is really possible. Their attempts and the attempts of those they know seem to back up this hopeless position.

The apostle Paul writes that Christ was made unto us sanctification (1 Corinthians 1:30). But many have no faith that He can do it through them, only that He can help them as they struggle. That's not an easy yoke; that's a hard one. That's not sufficient grace; that's insufficient grace. But that's all they have faith for, and it can only be done unto them according to their faith.

A hopeless heart limits the power of God that could be flowing out of our spirit into our soul and body. Andrew Murray, in his book *Abide in Christ*, says it this way:

> *Christ is made of God unto us sanctification. Holiness is the very nature of God, and that alone is holy which God takes possession of and fills with Himself.*[11]

Paul tells us in **Colossians 3:10:**

> **And have clothed yourselves with the new [spiritual self], which is [ever in the process of being] renewed *and* remolded into [fuller and more perfect knowledge upon] knowledge after the image (the likeness) of Him Who created it.**

God promised in Ezekiel that in the New Covenant He would give us a new spirit that would have the desire and ability for holiness.

> **A new heart also will I give you, and a new spirit will I put within you: and I will take away the stony heart out of your flesh, and I will give you a heart of flesh.**
> **And I will put my spirit within you, and cause you to walk in my statutes, and ye shall keep my judgments, and do *them*.**
> **Ezekiel 36:26–27** KJV

Maybe you don't feel like a new creation with God's law written in your heart, but it is there.

> **But this *shall* be the covenant that I will make with the house of Israel; After those days, saith the Lord, I will put my law in their inward parts, and write it in their hearts; and will be their God, and they shall be my people.**
> **And they shall teach no more every man his neighbor, and every man his brother, saying, Know the Lord: for they shall all**

know me, from the least of them unto the greatest of them, saith the Lord: for I will forgive their iniquity, and I will remember their sin no more.

Jeremiah 31:33–34 KJV

And I will make an everlasting covenant with them, that I will not turn away from them, to do them good; but I will put my fear in their hearts, that they shall not depart from me.

Jeremiah 32:40 KJV

God has promised not to turn away from us **or** let us turn away from Him. What a covenant! He does it all! The power to live for God has been stamped or sealed into our spirits.

It may not show yet but it's there. It is like the image exposed on photographic paper. It may not be visible yet, but it's burned in there. If you don't believe it, put the paper in the developer solution and watch the image appear.

The image of Jesus was burned into our spirit when we were born again. That image is appearing as we soak in His Word and His Spirit. With revival have come a lot of songs about rivers. The river symbolizes the Holy Spirit. Let's jump in! We need to soak in our Developer for His image to come forth in us. Revival will equip us for further revival. The deliverance is in the dance!

Separated and saturated

Real holiness is a **transformation** that God works in us. We position ourselves for this to happen in the preceding part of the dance—**obedience**. **Obedience**, as we have noted before, is in response to a **revelation**.

Revelation may be conviction. It may also be a call to worship, words to speak (often scripture), thoughts we are to meditate upon, or actions to take. **Revelation** is any way Jesus may be saying, "Here I am, come to Me. This is my heart. This is my passion. Step into the place I have for you now and my anointing (grace) will be there flowing through you as you **obey**."

When a **revelation** comes to show us more of the nature and character of Jesus, we see two images. It is like a double exposure. We see where He is and where we are, and those images don't line up. There is a contrast.

This is where **obedience** comes in. When we see the contrast, we are called to start moving toward Him. And when we line up in whatever way He leads, we are lining ourselves up for the grace of God to flow from our spirits into our souls.

In this process, we do become more like Him. His thoughts and feelings become ours. It is not so much a matter of imitation as much as assimilation. He is working through us but not without our full cooperation. Holiness is being "set apart." We separate ourselves unto Him. Then He saturates us with Himself.

We do the separating and He does the saturating. We do the insulating. He does the infiltrating. It's not enough to be separated (or insulated) from the world, the flesh, and the devil. We must be so saturated, so infiltrated with the Holy Spirit that worldly, fleshly things hold no attraction for us any more. In fact, we can be so full of the Holy Spirit that we constantly operate out of the overflow.

As we abide in Him, we bear fruit. We become the "sweet fragrance of Christ" to the world (2 Corinthians 2:14–15). First and always we seek Him. We rise up out of our darkness and move toward His light. When we in **obedience** get lined up with Him, the light of His holiness dispels the darkness in our soul.

Arise and shine

We arise and He shines—in and through us.

> **Arise, shine; for thy light is come, and the glory of the Lord is risen upon thee.**

> For, behold, the darkness shall cover the earth, and gross darkness the people: but the Lord shall arise upon thee, and his glory shall be seen upon thee.
>
> Isaiah 60:1–2 KJV

Although these words are about Israel, they can also be about revival in the last days all over the world. When the lukewarm church arises to seek God with our whole heart, the glory of the Lord will shine through us.

The prodigal son said, "I will arise and go to my father." Those in rebellion will come home. And the older brothers, the legalists, will come back from works to relationship. The Father waits for both. The prodigal can arise from his self-indulgent sin and come home. The older brother can arise from his self-sufficient works and join the party.

Mercy warns us to arise

The Parable of the Prodigal Son shows God as merciful and long-suffering. In contrast, the Bridegroom in the Parable of the Ten Virgins (Matthew 25:1–13) seems harsh. The ten were all to take care of their own lamps. Five did and five didn't. Time was suddenly gone, and it was too late for the foolish. They weren't even selfish or evil like the prodigal. The Amplified Bible calls these unprepared ones "foolish, thoughtless, and without forethought." Yet there was no second chance for a happy ending for them. Why? Is the nature of God different in these two stories?

No, but the dispensational times are different. God is merciful and long-suffering. That's why our Bridegroom is lingering. But the age of grace culminates with the second coming of Jesus. We are warned in this Parable of the Ten Virgins not to be presumptuous about the times because we don't know when Jesus will come back.

Grace equips us to shine

He's not trying to catch us off guard. He wants everyone that He died for. His heart is not just for us to be saved, but for us to have the privilege of helping with the harvest. If we arise, He can shine through us.

By the end of this age, the church, the bride without spot or wrinkle, will arise and shine as never before. The glory of God will be seen upon us. Yes, the enemy will throw out all he's got. But the darkness coming will be conquered by the overflowing power of the grace of God manifested through His people everywhere.

The harvest

Growing up in central Kansas, I was involved in many wheat harvests. Later in my life, God brought to my remembrance one particular harvest that was a picture of the end-time harvest of souls. The many analogies to the need for unity in the body of Christ are striking.

It had been a difficult, prolonged harvest that year, with more breakdowns of machinery and rain delays than usual. The remaining wheat bowed heavy and overripe in the fields. One more rain would make it too low for the combines to save, and the rest of the year's harvest would be lost.

We worked faster as the sky darkened and distant thunder signaled the beginning of the evening that would surely be our last chance to finish the harvest. ("The night cometh, when no man can work" John 9:4 KJV.) We finished with great relief, but realized that others were struggling against unbeatable odds—more work than time. We began to move our machinery into the field of a neighbor who was still cutting. When his field was all stubble, we looked at each other and said, "Who's still cutting?"

A growing number of men and trucks and combines moved from field to field, doing in a short time at each stop what would have taken one farmer many hours working alone. Were these really the same men who talk bad about each other in the coffee shop?

As I watched a line of different looking combines move slowly side by side across the last uncut field, the clouds went black, the air chilled, and raindrops began to splatter. Just before the storm hit full force, everybody's harvest was finally in and we all hurried safely home.

Fourteen

Prisons and Pedestals

or the enabling power of God's grace to flow from our spirits to our souls, our hearts must be kept clear of blockages. Since the heart is the connection between our spirit and our soul, the condition of our heart is tremendously important.

> Blessed *are* the pure in heart: for they shall see God.
> Matthew 5:8 KJV

This is not just about seeing God when we get to heaven, but it also has to do with our intimate communication with God *now*. We must guard our hearts with all diligence (Proverbs 4:23). Another scripture says that out of our belly (spirit) will flow rivers of living water (John 7:38).

We know sin can block that life flow. To avoid some subtle but dangerous blockages that are common to all believers, we must empty our prisons and pedestals. I cannot remember when it was or what preacher it was that gave me the *prison* concept about forgiveness. I wish I could give credit because this simple teaching, along with the *pedestal* idea that I added to it, has been very valuable to me. Sometimes it's hard to see our own spiritual condition. This chapter can give you a fresh clarity to deal with important issues we all face.

This is the definition of unforgiveness that has been so helpful to me. Unforgiveness is when we have someone locked up in the prison of our heart and we take them out from time to time and beat them up in our mind, remembering how terrible they were to us. Then we store them back in their prison in our heart for future times of mental flogging.

Releasing the hostages

Who's in your prison? Don't be too hasty to say nobody. There can be whole groups hiding in there. It's possible to carry a grudge against the kids you went to school with or the town you grew up in. Bad experiences can leave us with bad feelings toward groups of people by profession, such as lawyers, teachers, policemen, telemarketers, etc. Some people have even locked up whole races or genders because of repeated abuse by those in that category.

Who are the disgusting *thems* in your heart? Maybe this could include everyone richer or smarter or thinner than you? Even though you couldn't name names, you could possibly have multitudes locked up in your heart if you added up all the detested groups. Release all those hostages!

Jealousy is a jail keeper

Covetousness is a dangerous form of unforgiveness because it's not only resentment toward someone for being blessed in a way that we aren't, but it is also resentment toward God for supposedly blessing them more than us.

I thought I was not vulnerable to covetousness until I was in labor with my first child. After I had been in labor for nearly forty hours, I saw a woman being wheeled by on a cart in the hall outside my room. She was going in the direction of the delivery room and in a few minutes she was wheeling by in the opposite direction complete with baby in arms and rejoicing husband by her side.

I thought to myself, "How can she just whisk in here and have a baby? I've been suffering so long and may end up in surgery. Nobody should get to have a baby as easily as she just did."

I never met the woman, but a couple of days later I heard that she had recently lost her older child in a drowning accident. I was struck with guilt about my jealousy of her easy labor and delivery. I said, "Oh Lord, forgive me. She really deserved an easy birth." I sensed the Lord's thoughts back to me were, "So because she suffered sufficiently before, you will allow her this blessing now? If I carried her around on a pillow and let nothing bad ever happen to her all her life, what would that be to you?"

I was soberly reminded of Jesus' similar words to Peter in John's gospel. Peter, having just been told something about his own death, asked Jesus how John would die.

> **Jesus said to him, If I will have him stay (survive, live) till I come, what is that to you? [What concern is it of yours?] You follow Me!**
>
> John 21:22

We should not be distracted from our continual thankfulness by comparing our lives to others.

Mercy and grace

Let's go back to releasing our prisoners. Some people have themselves locked up. They may know they are forgiven but they have not received cleansing (see 1 John 1:9). So they continually berate themselves thinking, "I just can't believe that I did that! How could I have done such a thing?"

It may be painful to face our weaknesses, but it can work in our favor if we get a new revelation of our total dependence on Him. We can receive more of His grace (enabling power) so we will need less of His mercy in the future.

Mercy is not getting punishment that we deserve. Grace is getting the favor and blessing and power of God—which we also don't deserve. As we walk in more and more of His grace, we will need less and less of His mercy. But thank God, both are available.

Long distance dancing

Even God can be in our prison as we have discussed in previous chapters. Blaming God for bad things in our life can result in a distancing of ourselves from Him. Putting up walls of self protection between us and God is not so very different from putting Him in our prison, is it? It's a more passive-aggressive approach, but still an expression of resentment.

Doubt about God's integrity and goodness toward us is a major heart blockage. Ask the Holy Spirit to shatter any trace of that barrier. It's not only a faith killer, but it dishonors God.

Keeping the pedestal for One

Who else might be locked up in the prison of our heart? The ones who can hurt us the most are the ones whom we also love. Sometimes they are the ones that used to be on our pedestals. When they fell off our pedestals, we threw them in our prisons for a while and then let them out on the condition that they would resume their perfect position on our pedestal. They don't belong there either.

Only God is perfect and will always understand and never let us down. We have to empty our pedestal of everyone but Him. He is a jealous God. Anyone else in His place is an idol. Anyone or anything else we couldn't live without, if necessary, is an idol. Love and honor people, but as idols let them all fall. Have no other Gods before Him.

Having emptied our prisons, we let Him "contend with those who contend with us" (Isaiah 49:25). Having emptied our pedestals, we have only room for the One who will never hurt us. He is worthy of all our praise and all our lives.

> **If God is for us, who [can be] against us? [Who can be our foe, if God is on our side?]**
>
> **Romans 8:31**

We are in a battle but the fight is fixed. The deck is stacked. He's got us covered. We can rest in the shadow of His wings even as we fight, because no matter what happens we win. Here's a short poem the Lord gave me years ago about our safety in Him.

SAFE IN YOUR HAND
© by Margaret Westphal

God of my household,
God of the nations,
God of the last day,
God of creation,
God of my grandfathers,
God of my grandsons,
all of our battles You've already won.

Give us a vision,
show us our part.
We give You our lives,
we give You our hearts.
You're the Alpha and Omega,
the beginning and the end.
Surely You can keep us safe in Your hand.

Fifteen

Operating out of the Overflow

W e must be transformed before God can reach the world through us. We cannot transform ourselves. We can only get out of His way by giving up on our own strength and letting our weakness become a vessel for His strength. He can only fill an empty vessel. That filling not only will cleanse the vessel but overflow from us to others. The cleansing (**transformation**) is all God's doing but it happens out of our **obedience**.

> But in a great house there are not only vessels of gold and silver, but also [utensils] of wood and earthenware, and some for honorable *and* noble [use] and some for menial *and* ignoble [use].
> So whoever cleanses himself [from what is ignoble *and* unclean, who separates himself from contact with contaminating and corrupting influences] will [then himself] be a vessel set apart *and* useful for honorable *and* noble purposes, consecrated *and* profitable to the Master, fit *and* ready for any good work.
>
> 2 Timothy 2:20–21

We are potentially all vessels of honor. That means we can be "set apart," and "useful," and "ready" for any honorable and noble purposes the Master has for us.

We must not only be **in** Christ (or in the Spirit) but also **full** of the Holy Spirit. Staying in and staying full are both part of abiding. Jesus said, "Abide in Me, and I will abide in you" (John 15:4). There are two things going on here. Consider this diagram about being in Christ. The opposites named here are not intended to be all-inclusive or in any particular order, but just to give an idea of what it's like to be in the Spirit and out of the Spirit.

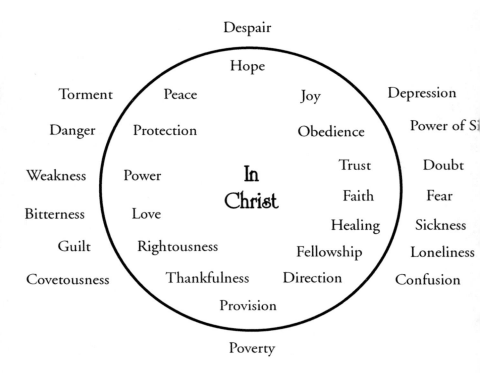

In Christ is everything we need, even if we're not receiving it all. Notice how the outside conditions could multiply and compound each other. But so can the inside things, the "in Him" conditions we find promised to us in the Bible. The circle in this "in Christ" diagram represents Jesus around us. Once we are in Him, we also need to be filled so we're not just separated from the bad, but also we are soaked in the good.

Here is another diagram to show how the staying in and staying full work together. Notice how the insulation and infiltration *both* are needed for transformation.

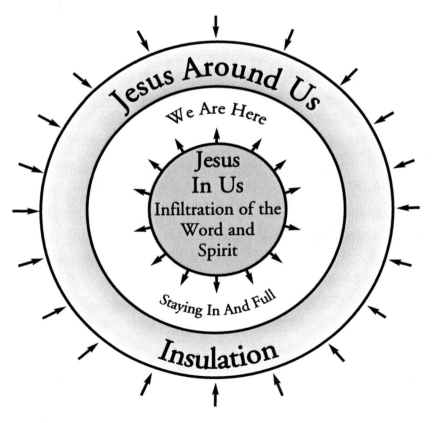

And thou shalt love the Lord thy God with all thine heart,
and with all thy soul, and with all thy might.
Deuteronomy 6:5 KJV

Does this sound a little extreme? Why can't we love God with
half our heart and love our family and other people with the other
half? When He said all, He meant all. He is a jealous God. When
He has access to all of us, then He not only can fill us, but He can
also provide an overflow for ministry to others.

When we give to others only out of our overflow, we'll never feel
depleted. What we give others should be from our extra portion
from God. This will help them much more than anything of ourselves. This overflow is not really from us, but Him loving people
through us.

This is essential for us too. We all have a need for love and affirmation. If this need is not totally met by God, we naturally look to
other people. We can become man pleasers instead of God pleasers
(1 Thessalonians 2:4). Then we are looking for the approval of people to prove our worth and give us happiness.

If our approval comes from God, then the approval of others
becomes optional. If the approval of others is optional, then we can't
be destroyed by their rejection. If we can be destroyed by their rejection, we give them too much control over us. Being too dependent
on the approval of others makes us want to control them too.
Without God, people play a lot of power games.

The more we operate toward others out of the overflow of our
relationship with God, the healthier our relationships with people
will be. It will be better for us and also for them.

Understanding all this in theory will not help us until we learn
to walk in it consistently. We can still get drained dry by all those
around us.

We can't overflow until we're full

Once, when I was feeling this way, I said to the Lord, "I understand what you showed me about operating out of the overflow. Why is it that I can't seem to do it consistently?" The Holy Spirit gently revealed to me that I didn't even have an overflow to give out of much of the time. This was because I cannot overflow until I am first full.

We have to stay full. It's a daily thing, this seeking God. His mercies are new every morning (Lamentations 3:23). We can't get by on yesterday's manna. Don't worry if you can't keep a set-aside time at the same time every day. If you can, that's great. If not, you can still fellowship with Jesus all day as often as you can.

Don't postpone prayer for some ideal time and setting. Would we starve physically because we didn't ever have time for a candlelight dinner? No, we gobble at stoplights and stash stuff in our desks. We don't ignore physical hunger too long. How much more important is our spiritual hunger.

Get hooked on the fellowship of the Holy Spirit. Talk to the Lord whenever you can as you work, walk, or drive. The Bible says to pray without ceasing (1 Thessalonians 5:17). How is that possible? When you get hooked on the presence of Jesus, abiding becomes natural and fun.

If you're hooked on caffeine, you don't just forget to get a cup of coffee. Get so hooked on Jesus that nothing else will do. He can become our passion instead of our religious duty.

I was teaching about prayer this way in a class one time and the next week a lady came back with an interesting report. She said that she actually was praying a lot more after getting away from the limited ideas she had about how and when she ought to be praying. She was enjoying continuous fellowship with the Lord instead of feeling guilty for not getting *the candlelight dinner* arranged each day.

I'm not advocating sloppiness in spiritual disciplines. I'm just emphasizing relationship over legalistic attitudes. We can get ideas and inspiration from hearing about what other people do, but we need to constantly be hearing from the Lord directly about how He wants *us* to pray and study the Bible. It will not be the same for everybody or for every season. **Seek** the Lord's will in this matter and He will give **revelation.** Then the important thing is **obedience,** not what that **obedience** looks like. He knows what is needed in each life for us to stay in the Spirit and full of the Spirit.

Then whatever He asks us to do for others is accomplished by the spillover of His love for us. Our leftovers should make others hungry for the source of our strength and joy. We are to be the salt that makes the world thirsty. If we've lost our savor, it's not for lack of giving out but for lack of filling up.

Jesus was constantly full of the Holy Spirit. He passionately pursued time with the Father even if it meant walking away from needy crowds. He understood about the overflow.

What Jesus gave to people was from the overflow of what He received from the Father. The love of the Father first came to Him and then poured through Him to others. His love for the Father was His primary motivator. He was so motivated to please the Father, that pleasing Himself and pleasing the Father were really the same thing.

The only real struggle was before the cross when He knew that final act of obedience would mean experiencing separation and rejection from the Father. What He was to face would not just be physically painful but spiritually horrifying. He would have to go through the anguish of being God-forsaken like us, so we could receive the kind of favor He had with God.

If God had compassion for us, then so did Jesus, because He and the Father had hearts knit together in love. However, I believe it was primarily His love for the Father that held Him on the cross. Yes, He knew He was dying for us, but first and foremost He did it for the Father and the overflow was ours.

God's wrath was poured out on God's Lamb and the overflow was enough to cover the sins of all men for all time! We don't have to fully understand it to be saved. We also don't have to understand *all* about how to grow in Him in order to grow in Him. The important thing is to keep pressing in, stepping out on what we do know. Staying **in** the Spirit and **full** of the Spirit, we can live overflowing with His grace and glory.

> As you have therefore received the Christ, [even] Jesus the Lord, [so] walk (regulate your lives and conduct yourselves) in union with *and* conformity to Him.
>
> Have the roots [of your being] firmly *and* deeply planted [in Him, fixed and founded in Him], being continually built up in Him, becoming increasingly more confirmed *and* established in the faith, just as you were taught, *and* abounding and overflowing in it with thanksgiving.
>
> Colossians 2:6–7

Conclusion

here's a holy hunger among God's people today. It's a hunger that only He can fill. It's a homesickness that will not go away until it drives us home.

Homesick heartache
to contain Your zeal again—
but my stiff cold wineskin
has no capacity for Your fire,
and my religious sensibility
scoffs at my desire
to leap into Your love and stay
where Your purity defines me
and Your faith flows
                    free from gray.

And the Spirit and the bride say, Come. And let him that heareth say, Come. And let him that is athirst come. And whosoever will, let him take the water of life freely.

Revelation 22:17 KJV

This scripture not only speaks of the second coming of Christ but also of the continual coming of Jesus to us. He's coming with continuous **revelation** and power as the scripture says, "full of grace and truth" (John 1:14). He comes in response to our continual **seeking** (as He draws) and our continual **obedience** (as He enables). Listen to this portion of the beautiful prayer Jesus prayed to the Father for us.

> I have made Your Name known to them *and* revealed Your character *and* Your very Self, and I will continue to make [You] known, that the love which You have bestowed upon Me may be in them [felt in their hearts] and that I [Myself] may be in them.
> John 17:26

Finding our place in Him doesn't happen by following some formula. It is a place of power born out of helplessness. We've tried to deal with our own sin and weakness and found that flesh cannot fight flesh, much less the devil. But neither the flesh nor the devil is any match for the Holy Spirit in us.

The Spirit calls inside and out. Our hunger turns to an aching emptiness that only He can fill. That emptiness becomes even like mourning, and when He comes He turns our mourning to dancing (Psalms 30:11). In Him we live, and move, and have our being (Acts 17:28).

In the dance is **transformation** that propels us on to **seek** with a purer heart and a deeper passion. We are ready to absorb more of His grace and glory. Our wineskin is ready to hold more of God because we have been stretched and softened by the Lion and the Lamb. More of the fabric of His being has been woven into ours so that we can hold more of Him.

Don't be afraid of losing yourself. **Matthew 10:39** tells us,

Whoever finds his [lower] life will lose it [the higher life], and whoever loses his [lower] life on My account will find it [the higher life].

You are not becoming less you, but more you—the real you—created in His image, for His glory!

Do you understand? Do you believe? Some things we must understand, but we can't until we take His hand and step into the purposeful abandonment of the dance. Herein lies the mystery of the dance.

> Passionate innocence—
> Your Spirit dancing with mine,
> saturates and softens
> my wineskin with Your wine.
> Jesus, You fill me with effortless trust
> and I'm splashing in Your laughter
> that washes me away
> to Your peace beyond my pain
> and into Your glory
>   past the gray.

The King of the universe, the lover of your soul, extends His hand to you saying, "May I have this dance for the rest of your life?"

Epilogue

In the fifth chapter of Ephesians we are told to be "ever filled" with the Holy Spirit. The next verse talks about psalms and hymns and spiritual songs and making melody in our hearts to the Lord. Worship can also be a sacred, silent soaking in His presence. That is such a beautiful, safe place. I found these words there.

SECURITY'S SONG
© by Margaret Westphal

I am alone but not afraid.
I am naked and not ashamed.
I am relaxed yet will not fall.
I need not strain to hear You call.

Hide me in the shelter of Your wings.
Fill me with the fountain of Your streams.
Swallow up the darkness in my soul.
Lightening of heaven, strike me whole.

Endnotes

CHAPTER THREE
1. Dr. James B. Richards, *Grace: The Power to Change* (Huntsville, AL: Impact Ministries Publication Department, 1993), p.12.

2. Mike Bickle, *The Pleasures of Loving God* (Lake Mary, FL: Creation House, 2000), p.58.

3. Dr. James B. Richards, *Grace: the Power to Change* (Huntsville, AL: Impact Ministries Publication Department, 1993), p.74.

4. *Ibid.*,p.9.

5. Attempting to contact the dead is strictly forbidden in scripture (Deuteronomy 18:10–11). The only moral and spiritually safe prayer concerning the deceased is prayer directed to God only. God will address whatever needs are brought to Him.

CHAPTER FIVE
6. Andrew Murray, *The Two Covenants* (Fort Washington, PA: Christian Literature Crusade), p.183.

7. *Ibid*,p.185.

CHAPTER NINE
8. Steve McVey, Grace Rules (Eugene, OR: Harvest House Publications, 1998), p.18.

CHAPTER TEN
9. Mike Francen, *Vision Passion and the Pursuit of God* (Tulsa, OK: Francen World Outreach Publications, 1995), p.72.

CHAPTER ELEVEN

10. Andrew Murray, *The Two Covenants* (Fort Washington, PA: Christian Literature Crusade), p.24.

CHAPTER THIRTEEN

11. Andrew Murray, *Abide in Christ* (New Kensington, PA: Whitaker House, 1979), p.62.

Suggested Reading

The writings of **Andrew Murray** have been a great inspiration to me in the last few years. His many small paperback devotionals are available in Christian Bookstores. He was a Scottish evangelist in the 1800s and so his writing style is not the kind you can read quickly and easily, but the insights he left for us are rich and beautiful and in no way outdated. Anything of his is valuable reading. I especially recommend *The Two Covenants* for studying law and grace.

Steve McVey has written three good books about the power of grace. They are entitled *Grace Walk*, *Grace Rules*, and *Grace Land*. Another strong contemporary teacher on the subject is **Dr. James Richards**, author of *Grace: The Power to Change*. **Dudley Hall**'s book *Grace Works* is very interesting too.

For specific information about the baptism of the Holy Spirit, I have found nothing more complete and articulate than *The Holy Spirit and You* by **Dennis and Rita Bennett**. It's a classic.

There are many wonderful books available about the power of God working in the lives of people in recent times. Two of my favorites are *Experience the Blessing* by **John Arnott**, and *Power, Holiness, and Evangelism* by **Randy Clark**. These are actually collections of various teachings and testimonies by a number of different writers.

The television ministry of **Andrew Wommack** from Colorado Springs, Colorado, has recently provided a strong confirmation for me that the concepts which the Lord has led me to communicate in *Spirit Dance* are important and timely. Andrew Wommack reminds me of Andrew Murray in his powerful emphasis of the need for believers to exercise total submission to and dependency on God. And like Murray, Andrew Wommack has an extraordinary understanding of grace, faith, and sanctification. Two good books of his are *Hardness of Heart* and *Living in the Balance of Grace and Faith*.

About the Author

Margaret Westphal and her husband Russell both grew up in central Kansas. Since 1990, they have lived in Tulsa, Oklahoma. They were married in 1971 and have three children who are now all adults living wholeheartedly for the Lord.

Margaret graduated from Rhema Bible Training Center in Tulsa in 1993. She and Russell, who is an architect, share an informal ministry of encouragement and hospitality to others. Margaret also has a passion for teaching, preaching, and writing about the love and power of God.

At the close of 2002, as this book goes to print, plans are underway to produce study materials that can be used with *Spirit Dance* for individual or group study.

For information about these materials, to order more copies of the book *Spirit Dance*, or to check out other information about the Westphals, see Margaret's website at www.margaretwestphal.com.